I0050332

THE FINANCIAL ADVISORS
BLUEPRINT
FOR SUCCESS

A ROADMAP TO UNLOCKING PEAK PERFORMANCE

INTERNATIONAL PEER GROUP

First Published 2025 by Ali Arayssi, Gail Singh, Hari Maragos, Jayang Nagrecha, John Fernandes, K. Venka, Kobus Kleyn, Kyriakos Chatzistefanou, Logan Naidu, Marta Kiraly, Miliana Marten, Mohamad Manmohan, Naji Haddad, Panos Leledakis, Plabita Priyadarshi, Priti Kucheria, Ravi Rajpal, Rima Antonios, Sandro Forte, Sepalika Panagoda, Dr Sijo Mathews.

Copyright © 2025 Ali Arayssi, Gail Singh, Hari Maragos, Jayang Nagrecha, John Fernandes, K. Venka, Kobus Kleyn, Kyriakos Chatzistefanou, Logan Naidu, Marta Kiraly, Miliana Marten, Mohamad Manmohan, Naji Haddad, Panos Leledakis, Plabita Priyadarshi, Priti Kucheria, Ravi Rajpal, Rima Antonios, Sandro Forte, Sepalika Panagoda, Dr Sijo Mathews.

ISBN 978-1-0370-441-3-7 (Print)
ISBN 978-1-0370-5579-9 (eBook)

Edited by Lee-Anne Weston-Ford

Cover Design and Interior Formatting by Gregg Davies Media (Pty) Ltd
www.greggdavies.com

All rights reserved.
No part of this publication may be reproduced, stored in or introduced into a retrieval system, or transmitted, in any form, or by any means electronic, mechanical, photocopying, recording or otherwise, without the prior permission of the publisher. Any person who commits any unauthorised act in relation to this publication may be liable to criminal prosecution and civil claims for damages.

Contents

Part Four

Client Relations and Trust Building

Part Five

Advanced Strategies and Adaptability

Part Six

Succession Planning and Futureproofing

Foreword
Tony Gordon

I am delighted to write this foreword to The Financial Advisor's Blueprint for Success. When invited, I readily agreed, recognising immediately the tremendous value and importance of this book to our profession.

Throughout my career, I have been fortunate to witness the transformative impact we financial advisors have on our clients' lives. Yet, achieving excellence as a financial advisor is no simple feat—it demands far more than technical expertise. It requires a profound commitment to continual personal and professional growth, genuine client care, and an unwavering dedication to ethical practice.

The authors of this book, a distinguished collection of some of the worlds most successful advisors, bring to these pages not only decades of experience but heartfelt stories and practical strategies that reflect the real essence of financial planning. They have generously opened their minds, sharing insights and proven techniques that promise to guide readers to greater success, regardless of where they are in their career journey.

Tony Gordon

What particularly resonates with me is the authentic and human approach each contributor has taken. This book is not just a manual, it is a conversation—a dialogue filled with wisdom that will inspire you to reflect on your current practices and encourage you to think bigger about what is possible. It demonstrates clearly that true success in our profession extends far beyond mere numbers or products. It hinges fundamentally on relationships, trust, vision, and action.

I know some of the authors well as fellow MDRT members and am certain readers will appreciate the practical guidance and inspiration contained within these pages. Whether you are starting your professional journey or seeking to enhance an already successful career, The Financial Advisor's Blueprint for Success is a timely and essential resource. Use it as a roadmap, a reference, and an inspiration. More importantly, apply its lessons thoughtfully and consistently. Success, as the book reminds us, is a skill we can all learn and refine through dedication and focus.

Congratulations to all the authors for crafting this outstanding guide. I am confident it will serve as an invaluable companion to advisors who aspire not only to achieve success but to positively impact the lives of those they serve.

Tony Gordon

MDRT Past President

Introduction

Unlocking the Blueprint to Success

Achieving success in this financial profession is never a matter of luck. It is built through deliberate actions, disciplined habits, and a constant commitment to improvement. This book, *"The Financial Advisor's Blueprint for Success: A Roadmap to Unlocking Peak Performance,"* is here to guide you along that path. It is a practical and inspiring resource for anyone looking to advance their career, whether you're just starting out or have years of experience behind you.

This is not just another book about providing financial advice. It is a culmination of decades of real-world experience, shaped by some of the most successful leaders in the profession. These contributors have faced challenges, celebrated victories, and made a lasting impact on their clients' lives. Their insights are designed to help you grow and succeed, no matter where you are in your journey.

The Core of the Profession

Being a financial advisor is about much more than understanding investments or analysing numbers. At its heart, it is about caring for people. Every decision you make has the power to shape your clients' futures, bring them peace of mind, and help them achieve their dreams. This book recognises the immense responsibility that comes with the profession, and provides the tools to help you rise to the occasion.

The contributors to this book are more than just successful advisors. They are innovators who have redefined what it means to excel in financial advising. Their stories and strategies will show you how to build trust, develop lasting client relationships, and deliver results that truly matter.

What's Inside the Chapters

Each section of this book focuses on a key aspect of becoming a high-performing advisor. From the basics of cultivating the right mindset, to mastering advanced strategies, the content is laid out to help you grow, step by step.

You'll explore how to engage clients effectively, establish trust, and refine your personal brand. These skills go beyond the technical aspects of advising, helping you form connections that are based on respect and understanding.

The book also examines how to transition from simply satisfying clients to delighting them. Creating those "Aha" moments builds loyalty and transforms clients into advocates who actively promote your services.

It doesn't stop at the present; it looks to the future as well. You'll find advice on embracing innovation, staying ahead of trends, and responding to changes in the profession. Whether it is adopting new technology or adjusting to market shifts, these strategies will keep you relevant and competitive.

Finally, the importance of legacy and succession planning ensures that the success you achieve doesn't end with you. Planning for the continuity of your practice and ensuring that your impact extends into the future are critical components of a lasting career.

Learning from the Best

The contributors to this book represent a diverse group of top performers from around the world. Their insights are not abstract theories—they are practical lessons drawn from years of experience. These exceptional advisors have faced obstacles, adapted to changes, and achieved remarkable success, and now they are sharing what they have learned with you.

These advisors don't just talk about what works—they show you how to apply it. Their stories and strategies will resonate with anyone serious about growing their career in the financial advisory profession.

Your Part in the Process

This book isn't just a collection of ideas—it is a call to action. Success requires more than reading; it demands effort, persistence, and the courage to take risks. The lessons in these chapters are tools, but it is up to you to put them to work.

As you read, think about how these strategies might apply to your own practice. Identify areas where you can improve and set goals for implementing what you have learned. Every step you take moves you closer to achieving your full potential.

Introduction

The Journey Forward

By the time you finish this book, you'll have a clear roadmap for success. You'll understand how to build a thriving practice, create meaningful relationships, and leave a legacy that reflects your dedication and impact.

The lessons in these chapters are not limited to financial advising—they are universal principles that can elevate any pursuit. Whether you are building a team, growing your practice, or contributing to your community, the strategies in this book will help you achieve excellence.

Success is a journey, not a destination. Are you ready to take the next step? The opportunity to unlock your full potential starts here.

Part One
Foundations of Success

Chapter 1
Six Success Secrets
Sandro Forte

Sandro Forte, FCII, FPFS, CFP, has received over 40 awards, including the Lifetime Achievement award for his contribution to financial services and philanthropy. He has raised over $28 million for numerous charities.

He is a renowned speaker and author (his book *Dare to be Different* is one of the bestselling books of all time in financial services), as well as a success coach, helping more than one million advisors across 95 countries become more successful. He has served MDRT in various leadership roles, including MDRT Foundation President.

Sandro is widely recognised for his innovative approach to business and his ability to inspire others to achieve exceptional results. His focus on ethical practices and delivering meaningful client outcomes has set a benchmark for the profession, making him a role model for advisors worldwide.

Beyond his professional accomplishments, Sandro is a passionate advocate for giving back, dedicating his time to mentoring young advisors and supporting grassroots community initiatives. His philosophy of "success through significance" continues to inspire individuals and organisations to create lasting, positive change.

Introduction

Success isn't accidental; it's a learned skill, just like any other that can be mastered in life. Before exploring the first of six success secrets, we must confront a fundamental question: Why do so many people fall short of their goals? It's rarely due to a lack of ambition—it's often the inability to act decisively and consistently that holds most people back.

This chapter focuses on the foundation of achieving success: cultivating a brilliant mindset. By shifting focus from conscious limitations to subconscious empowerment, we can unlock untapped potential and rewire our thinking. With actionable strategies and real-world insights, this chapter lays the groundwork for turning ambition into tangible results, paving the way for sustainable success in every area of life and business.

Developing a Brilliant Mindset

Before we look at Success Secret Number 1, let's first look at why most people don't achieve their goals. It's not a lack of desire; it's usually the inability to take action, for whatever reason. For most of us, goals are conscious thoughts we are often encouraged to write down or share with another person, thereby making us more accountable. Unfortunately, the conscious part of our brain is where the "little voice" lives, and it's the constant interference from this "voice" that leads to procrastination, excuses, and, ultimately, failure.

It has been said all goals should be "SMART" (Specific, Measurable, Achievable, Realistic, and Time-bound), but what's wrong with an unrealistic goal? One thing is certain: People fail in life, not because they aim too high and miss; they fail in life because they aim too low and hit! We may not necessarily achieve an unrealistic goal, but by setting it in the first place, we are statistically much more likely to achieve a better outcome than if we took on a task we knew we could achieve more easily.

So how do we achieve "subconscious success"? There are a number of ways, and one, in particular, tends to be effective for most of those who have a real desire to develop a brilliant mindset. We refer to them as *"Mind changers"*.

The process is simple: We first need to think of 20–30 goals that cover any aspect of our lives or businesses. These can be small, easy-to-achieve goals, or larger (unrealistic) goals. They can be short-term (something to be achieved in the next few days or weeks), medium-term, or longer-term.

Each goal needs to be written onto an individual postcard or plain piece of paper and written as a statement incorporating two specific "rules". The first is to write the goal as if it has already happened (i.e., in the past), and the second is to describe how we felt when we achieved the goal. For example: *"Appearing on the front cover of Health & Fitness Magazine was a testament to my dietary and training disciplines. I look and feel amazing."*

Having written 20–30 goals with an appropriate mixture of term length, size, and complexity, we then commit to reading each of the cards every day. The cards do not need to be studied or learned; we simply read them, put them away, and then repeat the same process every 24 hours.

When a goal is achieved, it should be replaced with another goal. Reading these affirmations every day "drip-feeds" the thought process into the subconscious part of our brain. Usually, within about 30 days, we start to experience some extraordinary results: We think differently, speak differently, act differently, and find others being attracted to us more readily than in the past. We exude confidence and positivity, and setbacks are seen as minor inconveniences rather than major obstacles.

We possess the ability to achieve anything we want to achieve, but to do so, we need to remember that the subconscious part of our brain does not know the difference between what is real and what is imagined, and so it has no filter. Whatever we learn subconsciously forms part of the habits we need to form, in order to remove conscious interference.

Establishing the Rules of Engagement

For reasons that remain a mystery, financial professionals have always seemed to adopt a degree of "subservience" when it comes to meeting —and advising—new clients. They seem to think clients need them more than they need their clients, and this is wrong. At each meeting, whether across a kitchen table or office desk, there seems to be an unwritten rule that only the prospective client has the mandate to "hire or fire". As a result, the advisor feels the pain of rejection when things don't go according to plan.

So, let's think about a different approach. On the basis that a good advisor has the ability to change a prospective client's life, there has to be a different strategic approach taken at the first meeting. By adopting a "you need me more than I need you" approach, the meeting should always start with the advisor establishing the rules of engagement:

> *"Mr/Mrs Prospect, I believe there are two reasons why we are meeting today. The first is to see whether we like, trust, and can work with each other in the future. The second is for me to see if I can help you. Of course, I'm not able to say with any certainty whether I can do that, but the quality of advice I am able to give you is based entirely on the quality of information you give me. Is that okay?"*

Let's examine what we have covered so far? Firstly, we have positioned things in such a way that we have let the prospect know, subconsciously, that the decision to work together is mutual. This means the prospect knows they can also be rejected, and as a consequence, there is a distinct shift in the relationship dynamic, even at this early stage.

The second thing we have done is to make the prospect accountable for the advice we might subsequently give, and in doing so, we eliminate the *"I'm not sure I want to share that information"* objection.

"Is that okay?" is a great three-word, logical question that advisors should use regularly to check the prospect's understanding or agreement to proceed. Since the advisor has established the rules of engagement, rather than the prospective client, this is also an opportunity to deal with anything else that may lead to an objection at some point during the process; for example, a prospect's poor experience with another advisor, economic uncertainty, costs and charges, age, inexperience, or anything else that may cause interference.

Dealing with these potential issues at the outset creates a sense of transparency and, in turn, helps the prospect to see the advisor as more trustworthy. Most importantly, it means the advisor remains proactive,

Sandro Forte

rather than reactive, throughout the advice process, and thus is always in control.

Effective Networking and Referrals

To start with, let's ask ourselves, *"What is a referral?"* Most would agree that a request for a referral (if successful) usually results in a name and telephone number. Unfortunately, this usually leads to a cold call, because we often find that the person we're calling knows absolutely nothing about us, or—just as challenging—doesn't even know the person who has provided their details?

Putting aside the fact that the word "referral" should be replaced with the words "personal introduction" (a name, telephone number, and personal introduction from the referring source to the new prospect), it has also been suggested the best time to ask for "referrals" is at the point of sale, since this is a time at which the client is most open to helping us grow our business. However, there is almost no statistical evidence to support the suggestion that this is the best time to be asking for referrals. In fact, asking for referrals at any time puts the client back in control of the process, and this is the reason we usually hear: *"I can't think of anyone right now,"* or, *"Let me think about it,"* or, *"I don't know anyone."*

If, as advisors, we provide the very best advice and service, should we really be asking for help growing our business? Similarly, if, as professionals, we are committed to providing a 360-degree, truly holistic financial service, we should be expecting introductions, and not be forced to ask for them. Rather than wait until our new clients are signing an application form, we should be addressing introductions during the first meeting, because there are two obvious opportunities that arise during our initial interaction with a prospective client.

8

Firstly, when we talk about the financial implications of death, we should, inevitably, be asking for details of guardians, executors, trustees, and beneficiaries. In most families, there are usually between four and eight of these individuals. Instead of asking to be introduced, we should be saying, *"I need to meet these people because..."* The reality is that if we are truly committed to providing a fully comprehensive service, we should not simply be focusing on the transaction at hand but also the much bigger picture, which includes long-term relationships and inter-generational planning. When a prospective client sees the value available to themselves and the people around them, they are far more open to providing the details of friends or other members of their family.

Usually, most prospective clients will have dealt with another professional person or firm at some stage, whether to buy or sell a house, in respect of a general legal matter, or for a tax-related service. If we seek to find out a little more about their experience of working with other professionals—and assuming it is positive—we have the perfect opportunity to contact that individual or firm.

> *"Hello, is that Mrs Smith? I have recently taken on Mr Jones, who I understand is also a client of yours, and he was very complimentary about the advice and service you have provided. Since I run a very successful financial planning business and frequently get asked by my clients for an introduction to a good lawyer/accountant, I wondered if I could buy you a coffee sometime and discuss the possibility of introducing you?"*

As with clients, when there is a potential benefit to another professional, the response is always positive. The other great thing about this approach is that we adopt the role of interviewer, rather than interviewee, because we need to ensure that this other professional will provide the same quality of advice and service we offer. As such, we need to ask lots of questions about their processes and standards, and the types of clients they already advise. Needless to say, we cannot guarantee exactly when they will refer clients to us, but over time, and in consideration of the principle of reciprocation, we will find out very quickly whether or not a good working relationship can be established, and if the third party is committed to helping us build our business too.

Consistent Process Implementation

So far, we've looked at developing a success mindset, establishing the rules of engagement, and getting more effective personal introductions. Another important principle of success is consistency; the more consistent something is, the more it is trusted. Unfortunately, the vast majority of advisors are not particularly clear in their process, which leads to deviation, a lot of wasted time, and unnecessary rejection.

Having already considered how we position ourselves with a new prospective client, we now need to support this with a robust process, because this is what leads to the client experience. Starbucks has not established itself as a renowned brand because of the quality of its coffee, any more than people go to McDonald's for a good meal. Their success comes from customers knowing exactly what they will get from the moment they walk in the door to the moment they leave. As financial planners, we should also be entirely clear and consistent with our own processes.

Though there are many examples, two methods to build better relationships can be introduced quite easily into the first (fact-finding) and second (presentation) meetings.

Before we start asking the fact-finding questions, we should always invite a prospective client to think about their ideal financial outcome.

Ask them to dream, to think big, and to imagine what life might look like if money were no object. Whilst, consciously at least, this will be hard for them to do, a bit of prompting will help. By engaging the right (emotional) side of their brain, we start to create a connection between their goals and objectives, and prompt a commitment to take action.

To help a prospective client's positive decision-making, we need to balance right and left (logical) brain thinking. It is simply not enough to emotionally engage with a prospect without giving logical reasons for taking action, any more than logical reasoning alone will lead to a desire to move forward. Whilst some of this "blue sky" thinking may not be something our prospects can achieve in reality, by setting a higher emotional bar, our job is to then introduce the logical reasons for taking action. This is where we talk about affordability, the cyclical nature of stock markets, and other good reasons to accept our recommendations.

At the presentation meeting, *"Three is key"* because when we present three different solutions (minimum premium, a level of cover required to meet the basic need, and the fully comprehensive solution), most human beings will instinctively eliminate one of the three options; in this case, usually the cheapest. Presenting three different solutions is not only a good way to increase the average case size, but also to ensure that more clients benefit from a more optimal level of protection or savings/investment. This will clearly demonstrate an advisor's commitment to true financial planning rather than recommending what a prospect thinks they need.

Delivering Outstanding Service

Most advisors will say they provide a "good" level of service, but what exactly is good? It's not enough to see clients once a year, believing a "one size fits all" approach is effective. A vulnerable client (someone who has suffered a bereavement, ill health, reached retirement, or sold a business, for example) inevitably has different requirements and expectations than someone who has a good deal of financial experience. Our reputation as advisors depends on one thing: Does the experience we provide match or exceed the client's expectation? If it does, our reputation grows. If it doesn't, then it diminishes.

Unfortunately, the one question most advisors fail to ask is: *"What does great service look like to you exactly?"* The word *"exactly"* is very important here because we want the client to be as prescriptive as possible in describing what they expect in the way of advice and service, moving forward. Some clients may want a lot more "handholding" in the early stages, whereas a city trader may prefer to call as and when required. When we know what great service looks like (exactly), we simply have to adapt our process to ensure we match, or exceed, those expectations.

This *"killer question"* is a simple but very effective way to grow our improving reputation and develop advocate clients.

Taking Decisive Action

At the age of 21, I was given the opportunity to join a financial services firm, and spent the first two years making lots of excuses for a lack of activity, feeling far more comfortable blaming others, the economy, and my manager, for my lack of success. I knew, deep down, that I needed to have a conversation with my stepfather Dave (my mother had remarried following the death of my father when I was eight years old), and though I knew it was the right thing to do, I still found having this conversation really difficult, believing I would be rejected.

My professional epiphany came on the 8th of December 1991, when I decided I would stop focusing on the outcome and instead focus on the process. I simply told my stepfather that it would be professionally remiss of me if I did not at least have a conversation with him about the life insurance I knew he needed. It was as simple as that, and to my great surprise, he said "yes".

Sadly, just a few months after Dave purchased his life insurance policy (becoming my first self-generated client in the process), he passed away from a very aggressive form of stomach cancer. So, whilst I was "thinking about it" (speaking to him), my stepfather was dying, and not a day has passed since then that I don't think about what might have happened if I had put off having the conversation for just another few weeks.

As he lay dying, Dave's final words to me were, *"Son, thank you for what you did for your family. I'm so proud of you."*

Though it was one of the worst moments of my life, Dave also presented me with a unique gift that day: *The realisation that the measure of one's success is not what we say we will do but rather what we do. Success is not enjoyed by those who sit and wait for the opportunity to make it happen.*

We can all learn success, just as we have so brilliantly learned to do so many other things that we now repeat, over and over, without thinking —like walking, talking, swimming, riding a bicycle, and driving a car. What we do about it, however, is a matter of choice, and so the obvious question is, *"What will we do to be successful?"*

Conclusion

By implementing these six success secrets, we can transform the way we approach our lives, businesses, and goals. Developing a brilliant mindset, establishing rules of engagement, redefining referrals, creating robust processes, asking the right questions, and taking immediate action, are all essential ingredients for success.

Success is not reserved for the talented or the lucky—it is a skill to be learned, practised, and perfected over time. The key lies in consistency, determination, and a belief that we are capable of achieving far more than we ever imagined.

Remember, the only limits are the ones we place on ourselves. It's time to raise the bar, take control, and make the most of every opportunity that comes our way.

Chapter 2
Activity is the Name of the Game!
Naji Haddad

Naji Haddad is a Lebanese financial advisor. A self-made, self-taught professional, he is determined to make a real difference by giving people access to a safer tomorrow.

Haddad studied economics and financial management, worked in banking, and later shifted his career to excel in financial advisory. As an MDRT Regional Chair, founder of Legacy Builders, and creator of BLIS—Beirut Life Insurance Seminars— Haddad provides coaching and motivational sessions to life insurance agents, worldwide. BLIS, a CSR initiative founded by Haddad, reflects his commitment to giving back to the community, and honours the legacy of his older brother Michel, whose belief in him inspired his career.

For Haddad, "Making money is good, achieving exceptional results is great, but nothing is more important than delivering a cheque to a client."

With two decades of experience, Haddad has provided financial backup to 800 families, alleviating their financial and emotional burdens during difficult times. Outside of work, Haddad is an avid traveller, biker, and life enthusiast. He enjoys self-improvement, nature, exploring the world for business and pleasure, and staying fit.

Introduction

In the life insurance profession, activity is truly the name of the game. Without consistent and focused activity, success will always seem just out of reach. As advisors and agents early in your careers, making activity a top priority and developing effective systems to maximise your efforts are crucial to building your business and achieving your potential.

In this chapter, we'll explore why activity matters so much, as well as highly actionable tips and frameworks for organising and optimising your sales activities on a daily, weekly, and monthly basis. By focusing on the right metrics and formalising your approach to prospecting, presentations, customer follow-ups, and more, you'll set yourself up for increased productivity and results.

Let's dive right in!

The Importance of Consistent Activity

In most sales professions, results are never achieved instantly. Selling life insurance is no different. It takes consistent, diligent effort over a significant period before the fruits of your labour materialise into closed sales and growing residual streams of commission income.

The key metric underpinning that growth is sales activity. Activity measures how many prospects you're contacting, presentations delivered, policies submitted, and so on. Maintaining certain weekly, monthly, and quarterly activity benchmarks tied directly to monetary goals gives you clarity on the work and systematic effort required to build your business.

Think about it this way: If your goal is to sell 25 policies per month, how many prospects might you need to engage with? Fifty presentations booked? One hundred initial discovery calls made? Those precursor activity metrics dictate what follows. Without understanding and diligently tracking those front-end figures, you'll struggle to create momentum.

Activity is also vital because generating leads, making contacts, and moving prospects through your sales process takes time and follow-up. Building meaningful relationships and convincing clients to buy requires multiple touchpoints and conveyed credibility over months or sometimes years. Without applying constant pressure through continual activity, those sales timelines drag out even further or go cold completely.

Finally, nothing replaces or shortens the in-person hours necessary to build a book of business. Elite life insurance agents, in time, become masters of their craft through trial-and-error learning applied across tens of thousands of conversations. As basketball legend Kareem Abdul-Jabbar once said, *"You aren't going to find the answers by looking at the floor. Keep your head up and your eyes open."*

Active participation over sustained periods is the only path to excelling in this profession.

For example, John, a new agent, made a commitment to make at least 50 discovery calls per week. Within six months, his consistent activity paid off—he had added 37 new clients to his book of business, significantly increasing his income. John's success demonstrates how diligently tracking and executing activity metrics can directly translate into tangible results.

Now that I've hopefully convinced you of why sales activity is a non-negotiable, let's outline some best practices for organising your efforts on a daily, weekly, and monthly timeline.

Effective Scheduling and Time Management

The first key to effectively managing sales activity is to form solid daily habits that focus your effort on one to two ideal activities at a time, rather than spreading yourself too thin. Attempting to juggle too many disparate sales tasks often leads to distraction and shallow results across the board.

Instead, devote each day to dominating just one or two stages of your sales process using systems and allotted blocks of time. For example, you might designate Mondays strictly to prospecting new leads, Tuesdays and Wednesdays to conducting discovery calls and delivering presentations, Thursdays to submitting paperwork, and Fridays to servicing existing clients.

Here's a sample schedule that organises sales stages across the business week while preserving non-negotiable self-care activities:

Monday: Prospecting Day

- **8–10am:** Gym, breakfast, prepare for the week
- **10am–12pm:** Lead generation
- **12–1pm:** Lunch away from desk
- **1–3pm:** Online prospecting
- **3–5pm:** Initial outreach calls

Tuesday: Discovery Day

- **8–9am:** Review schedule and objectives
- **9am–12pm:** Initial discovery calls
- **12–1pm:** Healthy lunch
- **1–5pm:** More discovery calls
- **5–6pm:** Process notes on prospects

Wednesday: Presentation Day

- **8–10am:** Gym, breakfast, prepare for the day
- **10am–12pm:** In-person presentations
- **12–1pm:** Quick, healthy lunch
- **1–5pm:** In-person presentations
- **5–6pm:** Debrief successful presentations

Thursday: Submit Day

- **8am–12pm:** Draft illustrations, process applications, and submit paperwork
- **12–1pm:** Healthy lunch away from desk
- **1–5pm:** Submit paperwork

Friday: Customer Service Day

- **8am–12pm:** Follow up on submitted applications, answer client questions
- **12–1pm:** Healthy lunch away from desk
- **1–3pm:** Continue follow-ups
- **3–5pm:** Commit to professional development

This allows you to apply maximum effort where it matters most each day while balancing prospecting, sales presentations, policy submissions, and customer service throughout the week.

Daily Activity Checklist:

- Plan and schedule your top 1–2 prioritised activities for the day
- Block out distraction-free time for focus work on those activities
- Set clear start and stop times to avoid burnout
- Take scheduled breaks away from your desk
- Log all activities and interactions in your tracking system
- Review daily activity metrics before ending your workday

Maintaining Motivation and Overcoming Challenges

Once you've established optimised daily activities and tracking methods, the next step is scaling up those metrics to support hitting weekly benchmarks, which accumulate into your monthly revenue objectives.

Taking our previous example, let's say your monthly goal is closing 25 policies at an average commission of $2,000 per sale, for $50,000 in overall volume. Pushing that down to the weekly level, you'd need to close around six cases per week. Thinking further upstream—if your closing ratio after delivered presentations tends to hover around 25%, you would then need to conduct roughly 24 presentations each week to achieve that weekly sales target more months than not.

Building on that figure, if your presentation booking ratio from discovery calls averages 50%, you would need to conduct approximately 48 initial discovery calls per week to feed into your benchmark of 24 weekly presentations. And finally, estimating that maybe 25% of discovery calls result in booked presentations, you likely need to prospect and contact around 192 new leads per week to drive 48 discovery calls.

While those figures are hypothetical examples, going through that deduction process for your own sales pipeline metrics allows you to quantify the weekly activity lift required to support attaining your monthly revenue goals.

The table below summarises the cascade effect in action:

Metric	Target
Monthly revenue goal	$50,000
Policies sold monthly	25
Policies sold weekly	6
Weekly presentations	24
Weekly discovery calls	48
Weekly new leads	192

Having clarity around the number of calls, conversations, and connections you need day to day, week over week, gives you targets to organise and assess your effort against. From there, it's applying systems around your sales workflow and prospect engagement, followed up by diligent daily execution.

Activity systems won't be a silver bullet overnight, but making them a habit over months and years is proven to pay dividends in the form of growing books of business and incomes for agents applying themselves. Keep your activity consistent, optimise as you learn, and track quantifiable metrics tied to sales objectives, and you'll be shocked at how making this the name of the game works to your benefit.

Power Prospecting

Let's start at the beginning with lead generation and identifying quality prospects. While referrals from existing clients and centres of influence (COIs) may support a level of sales volume, truly scaling your business over time requires mastering modern prospecting across both online and offline channels.

Power prospecting combines leveraging technology with old-school personal outreach and networking methods. Blend self-generated leads from tools like email outreaches and social media engagement with leads from brokerages, captive agency resources, and affiliated marketing systems. Develop lead sources both independently and through company-provided resources.

Building an initial prospect list is one thing—continually expanding it through dedicated lead generation time should be a weekly essential for any newer agent. Devote multiple hours per week to targeted prospecting campaigns across platforms like email outreaches on RocketReach or LinkedIn, Facebook community networking, cold calling, business event leads, and more.

Set a goal for adding 25–50 new leads into your pipeline weekly, then block off dedicated time to take actions that support that. For email campaigns, create customised value-driven outreach templates for different niche targets and set objectives for the volume of messages deployed per week. Treat social calls, cold calls, and events similarly by establishing consistent weekly goals for connections and conversations generated to fuel your lead funnel.

Leveraging the various available technologies and tools for the automation of processes for finding and engaging prospects at scale is vital. However, you want to ensure you customise messaging and approach contacts like real individuals rather than spamming the masses. Numerical prospect volume goals are important, but remember that prospects want to be seen and heard. Make use of automation but balance it with human focus and relatability when possible.

Take the case of Sarah, who leveraged LinkedIn and local networking events to continuously grow her prospect pipeline. Each month, she would connect with over 40 new potential clients through a combination of personalised LinkedIn outreaches and making valuable connections at industry events. This allowed Sarah to consistently book new discovery calls and sales presentations week after week.

In terms of offline networking, get involved with local professional associations, volunteer groups, industry events, community organisations, and more. Have a 30-second personal "elevator pitch", which explains your value proposition, dialled in for when you meet new contacts. Gather business cards, take notes on conversations had, and create reminders to follow up. Then deliver value and see if potential needs exist.

Dedicate time weekly to engage in a community organisation, or attend a local Chamber of Commerce networking event. Start conversations, find alignment and reasons to stay in touch, then execute polite, low-pressure follow-ups.

Phone prospecting still very much has its place for agents mastering connectivity with local small business owners, doctors, lawyers, and other niche targets. Set call volume goals and create customised scripts for different verticals you want to nurture relationships with.

A common theme you'll notice across online and in-person prospecting is needing to take the initiative, set weekly goals, and block off time on your calendar to execute these. Sales guru Jeb Blount breaks down his fanatical prospecting approach into a simple formula.

The Formula for Prospecting Success

$$FP = (L + C) \times A$$

F: Fanatical prospecting
L: Leads
C: Connections made through calls/conversations
A: Tenacious follow-up and consistency

Having lead sources (**L**) combined with proactive attempts to converse and connect (**C**) only works if you diligently follow up and sustain activity (**A**) over time to book presentations and close deals. This formula applies equally to online or in-person prospecting. Only committing to consistent execution yields results.

To build sustainable momentum, devote time daily to lead follow-up calls, emails, and requests to connect offline, centred around adding value and identifying needs. Resolve to contact 5–10 new prospects daily, in addition to engaging past leads. Set weekly goals for discovery calls booked, connections made, and presentations delivered, tied back to pipeline volume and monetary objectives. Fanatical prospecting principles put into practice multiply the probability of sales conversations.

In closing, approach power prospecting as a habitual ongoing journey rather than a short-term sprint. Leverage tools and technology balanced with authentic human engagement tailored to niche targets. Standardise weekly lead generation goals, execute daily prospecting tasks, continually expand your outreach methods, and nurture new relationships. Soon enough, the proof will be in the consistent quality presentations delivered.

Presenting Like a Pro

Now that we've covered reliable systems for building robust prospect pipelines, let's explore tactics to separate yourself when educating leads one-on-one or in group presentation settings.

Your outward confidence, subject matter expertise, and professionalism in delivering sales materials all make major impacts on how credible clients perceive the solutions you propose to be. While prospecting builds awareness and gets seats filled, patient education and clear value communication convert interest into sales.

Here are several highly actionable areas to focus on when it comes to delivering memorable and impactful sales presentations:

- **Know your materials inside out:** Practice alone until your core illustrations, product features, market landscapes, and unique selling points flow naturally. Memorise key talking points and statistics. Sounding competent inspires confidence rather than needing to rely heavily on slides.
- **Lead with values over products:** Sell the intangible emotions and protection your solutions provide rather than leading with policies or premium figures. Questions of "why" before "what" and "how" anchor conversations in people's deeper motivations.
- **Ask quality questions:** Facilitate two-way dialogue by asking open-ended questions to narrow in on root priorities, then layer logical solutions on top. Get prospects talking early and often.
- **Use visual aids:** Leverage illustrations, prototypes, and imagery to demonstrate functionality, and hammer home core messages. Simple yet professional slides, sample policies, and benefit guides all help.

- **Read body language:** Pay attention to prospects' non-verbal cues. Adapt messaging pace and tone to align with demonstrated levels of engagement and energy in the room.
- **Handle objections thoughtfully:** Welcome objections or concerns. They signal interest on some level. Address hesitations head-on with empathy while summarising benefits.
- **Manage group dynamics:** For multiple attendees, give space for questions, facilitate dialogue, and ensure all personalities feel heard. Draw out the dominant talker while coaxing quieter members to open up.
- **Tell stories that resonate:** Pepper in anecdotes that customers can relate to, which make products or services feel tangible and accessible. Stories stir emotions and linger longer than facts alone.
- **Clarify next steps:** Close every meeting, big or small, with clear expectations of follow-up timing and actions that advance prospects forward in considering or purchasing solutions.

Applying these tips will increase prospect engagement, reduce objections, and lead to more appointments booked and policies sold.

Sure, the initial product, pricing, and plan details that prospects want to understand, matter. However, leading with and circling back to the human elements of how recommended solutions improve quality of life compels decisions far more effectively. Practice leading from the heart as much as the head.

Submission Strategies

Now that you've expanded your prospect pipelines through power prospecting techniques, and delivered compelling presentations, let's discuss methods for expediting policy submissions while reducing obstacles that stall deals.

Preparation is half the battle when it comes to seamless policy submissions, especially with today's extensive documentation and inspection requirements. Compiling the necessary personal records, financial statements, existing coverage details, health histories, and beneficiary information ahead of applications makes clients' lives simpler amidst already stressful life events.

Provide crystal-clear instructions, laying out exactly which documents are required, and explain why scrutiny is applied. Set proper expectations that underwriting processes aim to validate and supplement information provided on applications with outside records. This prevents submission delays by ensuring everything is ready before starting the application.

Offer concierge-style assistance gathering records when reasonable if certain clients lack organisational skills or seem easily overwhelmed. Retrieving bi-verification records or doctors' visit summaries yourself shows helpfulness and protects commission payout timelines.

When completing applications, ensure clients fully understand each question before providing answers. Vet responses against past conversations to flag and clarify discrepancies in real time, particularly around secondary conditions or treatment profiles. Use pre-screening tools that identify common omissions such as foreign travel, medications taken, or dangerous hobbies. Get all pertinent facts on the table upfront.

Submit applications quickly upon signature to set verifications flowing and address potential delays early. Accompany submissions with summaries highlighting applicant strengths, such as financial health or favourable background details, to anchor positive perceptions from the outset.

Follow a submission checklist to componentise key tasks:

1. Pre-screen & prepare applications
2. Verify all documents enclosed
3. Review for accuracy & completeness
4. Submit & email carrier introductions
5. Schedule policy issue countdown calls

By mastering the art of submissions, you'll build credibility with underwriters and accelerate placements, benefiting both you and your clients.

Relentless Follow-up

If power prospecting sets the table, quality presentations serve the meal, and clear submissions clean the plates. Relentless follow-up is the cherry on top that completes client satisfaction.

Follow-ups and account management after the initial policy sale cement loyalty for repeat sales and referral business, fuelling long-term growth.

Use automatic triggers and reminders in your CRM to schedule periodic touches via email or phone with both your existing book of clients and recent closed deals. Send congratulatory e-cards for new policies issued, check in on milestones, and treat every service interaction as an opportunity for meaningful dialogue.

Discuss major life changes that may impact existing coverage or warrant needs assessments for additional products, such as marriage, promotions, or new children. Reinforce your commitment to providing lifetime value by proactively evolving with their financial needs.

At 90 days post-issue, reach out to reinforce that the selected policies were the right choice by emphasising the benefits realised since purchase. Ask for feedback and document positive responses for use as testimonials.

For group benefits clients, track open enrolment periods and initiate renewal conversations well in advance. Present proposals addressing prior pain points and provide midyear utilisation reports to demonstrate ROI on premiums paid.

The best time to request referrals or reviews is immediately following positive service interactions. Strike while the satisfaction iron is hot. Word-of-mouth recommendations carry more credibility than cold outreach.

When inevitable client issues arise, respond swiftly and with empathy. Focus on resolving the problem while validating their frustrations. Take ownership and communicate next steps clearly to regain trust.

Conclusion

Activity is the lifeblood of success in the life insurance profession. By committing to consistent prospecting, delivering impactful presentations, mastering submissions, and prioritising follow-up, you build a foundation for sustainable growth.

Make activity your daily mantra, track your metrics diligently, and apply systems that optimise efficiency. Success isn't achieved overnight, but you can unlock your true potential through persistence and constant improvement

Chapter 3
Vision Unleashed: The Key to Peak Performance
Logan Naidu

Logan Naidu is a distinguished financial expert, thought leader, author, and mentor with over five decades of global experience empowering individuals and organisations. A B.Com graduate, Certified Financial Planner® (CFP), and 44-year MDRT Qualifying & Life Member, with 12 Top of the Table and 22 Court of the Table qualifications, he exemplifies professional excellence, ethical integrity, and service.

For over 50 years, Logan has played a pivotal role in advancing the financial services profession, mentoring future leaders, and promoting professional standards through MDRT and the Financial Planning Institute of Southern Africa. His extensive leadership roles with MDRT culminated in his appointment as Divisional Vice President of the

Membership Communications Committee, MDRT Ambassador, and Chair of the MDRT Foundation's Global Engagement Committee.

A sought-after speaker, Logan has inspired professionals worldwide, delivering presentations on five continents, including multiple MDRT Annual Meetings. His 2015 Focus Session was translated into several languages. As a mentor, he has shaped the careers of many MDRT members and continues to influence industry professionals globally.

Beyond finance, Logan served 18 years on the board of Highway Hospice, participated in civic associations, and was actively involved in South Africa's anti-apartheid movement. A Vedanta Academy alumnus, his book, *Unleash Your Magic*, captures the essence of MDRT Annual Meetings, and reflects his insights on philosophy, spirituality, leadership, resilience, and personal transformation.

Married with three daughters, Logan divides his time between South Africa, India, and the UK, continuing his mission to uplift and inspire people worldwide.

Introduction

James Allen's profound insight: "*Man is the master of thought, the moulder of character, and the maker and shaper of condition, environment, and destiny,*" sets the foundation for this exploration of peak performance, both in the financial services profession and in life.

This chapter delves into the transformative power of visualisation, demonstrating how a clear, compelling vision can serve as the driving force behind extraordinary achievements.

The Power of Visualisation: Lou Tice's Impactful Message

Our journey begins with Lou Tice's powerful message on visualisation, delivered at the first MDRT annual meeting I attended in 1987 in Chicago.

Tice urged us to set clear goals and vividly picture them in our minds—not as distant aspirations, but as if we had already achieved them. At first, our vision and reality may seem misaligned, creating a sense of dissonance. However, the mind possesses an inherent drive to restore balance.

This is where our creative genius comes into play—working continuously to bridge the gap between where we are and where we envision ourselves to be. Each of us holds this extraordinary power to turn vision into reality.

Goal Setting and Achieving Peak Performance

The standard approach to goal setting often leads to an immediate follow-up question: *"How? How am I going to achieve this goal?"* In response, we begin listing the necessary resources, identifying potential obstacles, and considering the required effort. But this process can be overwhelming. The sheer magnitude of the task may tempt us to compromise, lowering our goals before we even begin.

Instead, we must resist the urge to ask *"how"*. Do not concern yourself with how the goal will be achieved—simply visualise it with clarity and conviction. Trust that the *"how"* will reveal itself in due course. The key is to remain unwavering in your goal. If you compromise, your subconscious mind will fail to fully commit, diminishing your drive to attain it.

But how does this process work? The answer lies in the **reticular activating system (RAS)**, a network at the base of the brain responsible for filtering information. It is like an executive assistant, meticulously sorting through vast amounts of data and passing only the most relevant information to the CEO—your conscious mind.

Consider a bustling household filled with background noise: street traffic, airplanes overhead, loud music from teenagers. Amid this chaos, a mother sleeps soundly—until her baby stirs. Though the baby's cry is far quieter than the surrounding noise, it instantly rouses her. Why? Because the sound holds value to her subconscious mind. It is the value, not the volume, of the information that is important, and that makes all the difference.

Similarly, when we set a clear and unwavering goal, our RAS begins filtering in opportunities, connections, and resources that align with it —while discarding distractions. This is the power of quantum thinking: We break free from conventional limitations and tap into our creative genius, embracing the vast possibilities of the mind. When we do this, we no longer react to life—we create it.

We hold within us the power to shape the future.

A Pivotal Year: Applying the Power of Visualisation

At that time, I was hungry for ideas and knowledge, eager to learn from the best. Louis Tice, a renowned motivational speaker, was a force of inspiration. His words resonated deeply with me, not just because of his reputation but because they carried the weight of experience and wisdom. I was determined to apply what I learned.

So, what did I do next? I took immediate action!

Albert Einstein once said, *"Imagination is everything. It is the preview of life's coming attractions."* By silencing the *"how"* and embracing the limitless potential of the mind, we activate the **reticular activating system**—the mental filter that directs our focus towards goal attainment.

The year 1987 was a defining moment for me. Inspired by Tice's insights, I set an audacious goal: to qualify as one of my company's **top 25** advisors. Visualisation became my driving force. I saw the achievement clearly in my mind—I felt it, believed it, and made it real in my thoughts long before it materialised.

At the end of that production year, after the official results were announced, I took a bold step. I sent a card to each of the top 25 qualifiers, congratulating them on their success. But I didn't stop there. I added a declaration—one that would hold me accountable to my vision:

> *"Sincere congratulations on qualifying for the Top 25. Enjoy the trip. I will join you for next year's Top 25 trip."*

With that simple yet powerful act, I had set my intention in motion. The path was unfolding—one visualisation at a time.

Real-life Success Stories

Following Louis Tice's advice, I ignored the *"how"* and focused entirely on visualisation. I vividly imagined my wife and myself on the Top 25 trip to Singapore and Hong Kong—destinations I had never visited. My mental imagery became so real that it blurred the line between aspiration and reality. I envisioned walking into a Hong Kong shop and purchasing a Sony 8mm video recorder, a luxury item at the time. These detailed visualisations, repeated with conviction, created a fascinating effect; my subconscious began treating them as actual experiences, triggering the mind's natural drive to align reality with expectation.

The result? I not only secured a place in Southern Life's Top 25, but I did so repeatedly, year after year. Even more remarkable—a few of us actually bought Sony 8mm video recorders in Hong Kong, just as I had visualised. This was not mere coincidence—it was proof. **Visualisation is not just a theory; it is a tested and repeatable practice.** If you believe and act with conviction, extraordinary success is inevitable. The only true limits are the ones we impose on ourselves. Despite our ordinary nature, each of us holds the capacity for extraordinary achievements.

This principle was reinforced when I was invited to motivate a struggling soccer team on the brink of relegation from the South African Premier League. The situation was dire—seven matches remained, the team was at the bottom of the log, morale was shattered, and huge financial losses loomed. The harsh reality: 27 matches played, 16 losses, and a negative goal difference of 18.

Before a crucial match, I conducted a one-hour session with the team at the Umhlanga Hotel. The players arrived looking drained and demoralised. I knew I had to shift their energy. **Laughter** became the catalyst. I used humour to break the tension, and the mood lifted almost instantly. With the atmosphere transformed, I led them through a detailed visualisation exercise—not just imagining victory but specifying the winning margin. Enthusiasm soared, and a few players boldly declared a 10-0 win! Others were more cautious, and we eventually agreed on a 4-0 target.

It was a lofty goal, but an achievable one.

That evening, the match remained scoreless at halftime. The pressure was mounting, and relegation was a looming threat. At the break, I gathered the team for one last mental reset. Twenty minutes from the end, the breakthrough came—a goal, at last! The momentum shifted, and soon after, they scored two more. Then, in a stunning turn of events, a fourth goal sealed the match. The team had achieved exactly what they had visualised. But the story didn't end there. In the dying moments, an own goal from the opposition pushed the final score to 5-0 —exceeding even their ambitious expectations!

This unexpected victory became a turning point. With renewed confidence, and more motivational sessions, the team surged forward, winning four of their last six matches, drawing one, and losing just once. Their +8-goal difference in those final games proved decisive, securing their place in the Premier League.

This experience solidified an undeniable truth: **visualisation is a powerful force, capable of reshaping reality.** With belief, focus, and action, even the most daunting challenges can be overcome.

Visualisation in Action: Lessons from the Greats

Many of the world's most successful individuals credit visualisation as a key driver of their achievements.

Arnold Schwarzenegger, a six-time Mr Universe winner, visualised his victories long before they became reality. He imagined himself holding the trophy, walking with confidence, and ultimately winning. Later, he applied the same technique to his Hollywood career, seeing himself as a successful actor before it materialised.

Neeraj Chopra, India's first Olympic gold medallist in track and field, repeatedly visualised his javelin throws in the Tokyo Stadium before he even arrived. By mentally rehearsing the setting and competition, he eliminated nervousness and heightened his performance.

Oprah Winfrey attributes her breakthrough role in *The Color Purple* to visualisation. She encourages others to *"create the highest, grandest vision"* for their lives, believing that what we see and believe, we achieve.

Tennis legends **Serena Williams** and **Rafael Nadal** used visualisation to mentally play out their matches before stepping onto the court. **Michael Phelps** and **Katie Ledecky**, both Olympic swimming icons, visualised every stroke, feeling the water and pace in their minds before each race.

Jim Carrey, once a struggling actor, famously wrote himself a check for $10 million for *"acting services rendered."* Years later, he landed a role in *Dumb and Dumber*—earning exactly that amount.

As **Michelangelo** once said, *"The greater danger for most of us lies not in setting our aim too high and falling short; but in setting our aim too low, and achieving our mark."* **Dream big. Visualise success. Then make it happen.**

The Role of Visualisation in Achieving Peak Performance

The power of visualisation in peak performance is well documented, with insights from leading experts like **Dr Charles Garfield**, whose PhD research focused on the habits of high achievers. His findings were clear:

"Virtually all athletes and other peak performers are visualisers. They see it, feel it, and experience it before they do it," asserts Dr Garfield.

This concept was further reinforced by **Gil Eagles** at an MDRT annual meeting, where he emphasised our innate ability to reshape our mental imagery and unlock the potential of the subconscious mind.

Logan Naidu

"We humans have the incredible capacity to change the pictures in our minds," Eagles proclaimed.

The message is unmistakable—**embrace discomfort, persist through failures, and most importantly, take action**. The timeless mantra **"Just do it!"** is more than a slogan; it encapsulates the mindset required for extraordinary success.

Timeless wisdom echoes this truth. **James Allen**, in his classic work *As a Man Thinketh*, profoundly observed:

> *"You are today where your thoughts have brought you; you will be tomorrow where your thoughts take you."*

Similarly, **William James**, often regarded as the father of modern psychology, emphasised the transformative power of sustained visualisation:

> *"There is a law in psychology that if you form a picture in your mind of what you would like to be, and you keep and hold that picture there long enough, you will soon become exactly as you have been thinking."*

These enduring insights affirm a fundamental principle: **the mind shapes reality**. By harnessing the power of visualisation, we don't just set goals—we create the future.

Conclusion

This chapter, *Vision Unleashed: The Key to Peak Performance*, underscores the transformative power of visualisation for those striving for excellence—whether in your profession or in life.

Far from being a technique reserved for athletes or actors, visualisation is a fundamental practice with the potential to shape the journey of financial professionals and high achievers in any field. By crafting vivid mental images of success, aspiring MDRT Top of the Table members immerse themselves in a future where they have already achieved their goals. This practice erases the gap between aspiration and reality, reinforcing belief and aligning actions with vision.

At the heart of this process lies the reticular activating system (RAS)—the mind's gatekeeper—which filters relevant information to support one's goals. The success stories of Michael Phelps, Oprah Winfrey, Neeraj Chopra, Arnold Schwarzenegger and others highlight how visualisation serves as a catalyst for peak performance.

Ultimately, this chapter affirms that **visualisation is not merely a mental exercise—it is a powerful tool for unlocking dormant potential and achieving extraordinary success**. When practiced with conviction, it transforms dreams into reality, proving that **the mind truly shapes our destiny**.

Part Two
Client Acquisition Strategy

Chapter 4
Prospecting Call Preparation Strategies
Mohamad Manmohan

With nearly 40 years' experience, Manmohan has consistently demonstrated a commitment to excellence and leadership. Throughout his career, he has been honoured with every major award in the profession, reflecting his dedication and exceptional performance.

He takes pride in mentoring individuals and teams who have achieved remarkable success. His track record includes the highest number of MDRT (Million Dollar Round Table) qualifiers over the years, showcasing his expertise in driving results and fostering a culture of achievement.

As a sought-after speaker, Manmohan has shared his insights on various platforms, locally and internationally, inspiring professionals to reach new heights in their careers. His dynamic presentations combine practical strategies with motivational techniques, leaving audiences equipped and energised to excel.

Beyond his professional achievements, Manmohan is passionate about giving back to the profession. He remains dedicated to empowering others and contributing to the growth of the insurance profession, firmly believing in the need to spread awareness and drive positive change.

Preparing for Prospecting Calls

Prospecting, the process of identifying and cultivating potential customers, is a critical aspect of our business. However, it can often be a challenging and time-consuming task. Fortunately, with the advancements in technology and the availability of various tools and resources, prospecting in our field has become easier and more efficient than ever before. From social media platforms and customer relationship management (CRM) software to data analytics and lead generation tools, we now have a wide array of options to streamline our prospecting efforts. This has not only made prospecting more accessible but has also enabled our business to identify and connect with potential customers in a more targeted and personalised manner.

Challenges

We often face several common challenges when prospecting for clients. Some of these challenges include:

1. **Identifying high-quality leads**: One of the primary challenges for us is identifying high-quality leads. Finding potential clients who are genuinely interested in life insurance and have

the financial means to purchase a policy can be a time-consuming and challenging process.

2. **Accessing the target market**: Identifying and accessing the target market can be a challenge, especially for those who are new to the profession or operating in a competitive market. Finding effective channels to reach potential clients and engage with them can be a significant hurdle.

3. **Lack of prospecting skills**: Not all of us have the necessary prospecting skills to effectively identify, engage, and convert potential clients. Developing and honing prospecting skills is a common challenge for many in our profession.

4. **Building trust and credibility**: Establishing trust and credibility with potential clients can be difficult, especially in a profession where scepticism and misconceptions about life insurance are prevalent. Overcoming negative perceptions and building trust with potential clients is a significant challenge.

5. **Overcoming rejection**: Prospecting often involves facing rejection from potential clients. Dealing with rejection and maintaining a positive mindset can be challenging, especially when faced with a high volume of rejections.

6. **Differentiating from competitors**: The life insurance profession is highly competitive, and we must differentiate ourselves from competitors to stand out. Communicating our unique value proposition and demonstrating why potential clients should choose us over other professionals can be a significant challenge.

7. **Compliance and regulatory requirements**: We must navigate complex compliance and regulatory requirements when prospecting for life insurance clients. Ensuring that our prospecting activities adhere to industry regulations and legal standards can be a challenging aspect of the process.

8. **Time management**: Prospecting requires a significant investment of time and effort. Balancing prospecting activities with other responsibilities, such as client servicing and administrative tasks, can be a challenge.

9. **Adapting to changing consumer behaviour**: Consumer behaviour and preferences are constantly evolving, particularly in the digital age. We must adapt to changing consumer behaviour and preferences to effectively prospect for clients.

10. **Generating referrals**: While referrals are a valuable source of leads, generating consistent, high-quality referrals can be a challenge for many. Building a robust referral network and incentivising clients to provide referrals requires strategic effort and relationship building.

Strategies and Techniques

Addressing these common challenges requires a strategic and proactive approach. By understanding and addressing them, we can enhance our prospecting efforts and achieve greater success in building a strong client base in the life insurance profession.

Here are some strategies and techniques to make prospecting easier, in order to enhance your client base and drive business growth:

1. Understanding the target market

One of the first steps in making prospecting easier in our profession is to understand the target market. This involves conducting thorough market research to identify the demographics, needs, and preferences of potential clients. By understanding the target market, we can tailor our prospecting efforts to resonate with the specific needs and concerns of potential clients, making it easier to engage with them and build meaningful relationships.

One of the easiest ways to get this work off the ground is to use a mobile phone directory. Start by organising your contacts into different categories or segments based on your relationship with them or their potential as prospects. For example, you could create segments for policyholders, family, colleagues, acquaintances, and potential business leads.

Once you have segmented your contacts, you can prioritise the segments based on their potential as prospects. For example, you might prioritise potential business leads over friends and family.

After prioritising your segments, you can then create a sequence for reaching out to each segment. This could involve setting specific times to call or message each segment and planning out a series of touchpoints to gradually build rapport and interest.

By organising your contacts and creating a sequence for reaching out to them, you can overcome prospecting fear, and make the process more manageable and effective, as the names in your mobile phone directory are known to you.

2. Utilising data and technology

In today's digital age, data and technology play a crucial role in making prospecting easier. We can leverage data analytics and customer relationship management (CRM) systems to identify potential leads and track customer interactions. By utilising technology, we can streamline our prospecting efforts, identify high-potential leads, and personalise our approach to engaging with potential clients more effectively.

3. Networking and referrals

Networking and referrals are powerful tools for making prospecting easier. Building strong relationships with existing clients, industry professionals, and community members can lead to valuable referrals and introductions to potential clients. By actively participating in industry events, networking groups, and community activities, we can expand our reach and access a steady stream of high-quality leads through referrals.

4. Educational workshops and seminars

Hosting educational workshops and seminars can be an effective way to make prospecting easier. By providing valuable information and insights on topics relating to life insurance, retirement planning, and financial security, we can position ourselves as trusted advisors, and attract potential clients who are seeking guidance and expertise. Educational events also provide an opportunity to engage with potential clients in a non-sales environment, fostering trust and credibility.

5. Content marketing and thought leadership

Content marketing and thought leadership can significantly enhance prospecting efforts. By creating and sharing valuable content such as blog posts, articles, and videos on topics relevant to life insurance and financial planning, we can establish ourselves as industry experts, and attract potential clients who are seeking information and guidance. Thought leadership content can also help us stay top of mind with potential clients, making it easier to initiate conversations and build rapport.

6. Segmentation and personalisation

Segmentation and personalisation are key strategies for making prospecting easier. By segmenting potential clients based on their demographics, life stages, and financial goals, we can tailor our prospecting approach to address the specific needs and concerns of each segment. Personalised communication and offerings can significantly enhance engagement and conversion rates, making prospecting more efficient and effective.

7. Utilising social media and online platforms

Social media and online platforms offer valuable opportunities for making prospecting easier. We can leverage social media platforms such as LinkedIn, Facebook, and X to connect with potential clients, share valuable content, and engage in meaningful conversations. Online platforms such as industry forums, community groups, and online marketplaces also provide avenues for reaching potential clients and building relationships in a digital environment.

8. Continuous learning and skills development

Continuous learning and skills development are essential for making prospecting easier in our profession. We should invest in ongoing training and development to enhance our prospecting skills, stay updated on industry trends, and learn new techniques for engaging with potential clients. By continuously improving our prospecting capabilities, we can adapt to changing market dynamics and stay ahead of the competition.

Preparing Mentally to Make Prospecting Calls

1. Always remember, it is only a conversation

All you are doing is talking to somebody. Far too many financial advisors put an unnecessary amount of stress on the phone calls they have to make. No, you are not going to solve some big family dispute, nor are you going to solve some major national crisis. It is just a conversation, so relax. Some of your conversations will go well, and some will not. That is fine.

2. Know your objective

Before you make the phone call, know what your objective is. Often, advisors think they are going to go all the way to close the case. Unless you are dealing with a very simple matter, that won't happen. On the call, you're just going to do two things: first, secure one piece of information; next, set a date and time for a follow-up meeting. Chances are that the person didn't expect your phone call and honestly doesn't have time for a long discussion. Know your objective before you make the call.

3. Create success in others

Your goal is to help the prospect prepare for their future. When we educate a prospect, this is what we do. Whenever we close a deal, we are creating a secure future for the prospect and their family. When you prospect, you are starting another person on that journey towards security. That should excite you. It excites me! Whenever I make a prospecting call, I am beginning someone on a path to total security.

4. Mind games

Your mind plays incredible games against you and tells you why you cannot do something. In your head, you might hear: "Oh, you can't do this. Oh, you can't." That is not true. Then, your mind will tell you: "Oh, you need to take care of this customer," or "You need to do this. Take care of this." Your mind will always tell you everything you need to do except prospect. You end up being busy, but not productive. It needs to be your goal to turn that negative prospecting mindset into a positive one.

How do you do that? Look at all your current customers and note how you have helped them achieve success. Remind yourself that this is the reason why you prospect. When we prospect, we help people with their futures. Think through the people, companies, and families you have helped. That will help you take your negative mindset and turn it into a positive one.

5. Set goals you can achieve

Too often, I see people set unattainable goals. For instance, saying, "My pipeline is empty, so I need to fill it within 30 days." Trust me, that won't happen. Set goals that you can achieve. If you are struggling with prospecting, set yourself very simple goals. Maybe you aim to make just 10 prospecting calls today. That's it! Once you get over that hurdle, you can increase it to 20 and gradually make more calls. Momentum creates momentum, and that will work to your advantage.

6. Work your plan

Often, advisors will prospect a little but then give up if it doesn't work immediately, trying something else instead. Stick with your plan, because the results of prospecting don't occur on the first call. The results from prospecting occur further down the line.

I like to use the analogy of a farmer. He plants seeds and comes back a week later; nothing is growing. He doesn't give up or complain but continues planting more seeds. A few weeks later, he notices growth, but there's nothing to harvest yet. Every farmer knows they must wait for the harvest. Prospecting is similar. You won't get results on the first few calls. The results will come on the 10th, 11th, or 12th call. You've got to work your plan.

7. Leverage your time

If you don't leverage your time, your time will leverage you. If you keep saying, "I'll prospect tomorrow," you may end up spending all day planning or preparing and never actually making calls.

Leverage your time by breaking it down into three windows:

- Planning to prospect
- Preparing to prospect
- Actually prospecting

The first two steps are crucial, so that when it's time to prospect, you're ready to make calls and get the job done.

8. Know your outcome

Look at your current policyholders to see the outcomes they've achieved. This isn't about what you sold them; it's about what they've achieved because of your relationship with them. When you know your outcome, you'll be more confident in asking the right questions and having productive conversations.

9. Peer support

Sales is not a solo activity—it's a team sport. Peer support is essential. Surround yourself with people who motivate you, hold you accountable, and celebrate your successes.

10. Motivation and celebration

It's not your leader's job to motivate you. Motivation comes from within. Celebrate your wins, no matter how small. Even securing a phone number or setting up a meeting is a success. Celebrate every step, as these wins will build your confidence and drive your journey towards success.

Conclusion

Prospecting is a fundamental aspect of our profession, and making it easier requires a strategic and proactive approach. By understanding the target market, leveraging data and technology, utilising networking and referrals, hosting educational events, creating thought leadership content, segmenting and personalising prospecting efforts, utilising social media and online platforms, and investing in continuous learning, we can enhance our prospecting capabilities and drive business growth.

With the right strategies and techniques in place, prospecting can become a more efficient and rewarding process, enabling us to build a strong client base and achieve long-term success in the life insurance profession.

Chapter 5
Core Practices of Successful Insurance Professionals
Plabita Priyadarshi

Plabita Priyadarshi is a recognised leader in insurance and investment consulting. As the top advisor at Kotak Life Insurance since 2005, she was named one of India's top 100 women in finance for 2019 by AIWMI. Her achievements include the title of International President of the 51 Club, and honours from Old Mutual in South Africa.

She has been inducted as a "Living Legend" in the Advisors' Hall of Fame every year since 2015, and is a 17-time Kotak Platinum Club qualifier. A dedicated MDRT member since 2005, Plabita has achieved six TOT, nine COT, and four MDRT qualifications. She has also served in key leadership roles for MDRT, including as India's "Country Chair" and member of several task forces.

Plabita is an inspiring speaker, addressing events like MDRT's focus session in Miami on post-retirement financial planning, and the 2019 MDRT Day India. Her journey from fashion to finance has been featured in YourStory and Kotak Life Insurance publications.

Her philosophy of "proving the odds wrong" reflects her belief in resilience and commitment as the foundations of success, guiding her to professional and personal fulfilment.

Introduction

In the era of unlimited information and technological advancement, the insurance profession, like many other professions, has also changed, and the dynamics are very different. To be successful and remain in the business of insurance, it's important to follow some of the core practices listed below:

Consistency in prospecting and face-to-face appointments

Anybody working in this profession should focus on two of the activities that generate the most revenue. One is continuous prospecting, and the other is regular face-to-face appointments. All of us know that there is a ratio behind everything. The bigger the number, the higher the chances of success in business.

Some of the prospecting techniques that help with getting prospects regularly are:

- **Cold calling** – This technique entails contacting a prospect directly. Though there is the potential for rejection, if this process is done with good preparation in a known pool, one can achieve good results. Follow-up calls and connections are essential.

- **Cross-selling** – This is a highly reliable way to increase your success with prospecting. Your clients are already known to you. Regular reviews, e.g., 100 days after the first sale and 100 days prior to the policy's anniversary, increase the chances of repeat business.
- **Referral programs** – References from known people and existing clients can increase the number of available prospects. It is important to maintain a connection with the person providing you with these references.
- **Prospecting dinners, group/corporate presentations, social media activity, and direct mailers** – These are additional ways to gain prospective clients.

Another important aspect is daily face-to-face appointments. To be consistent, it is important to meet at least one prospect daily and explain the solutions you can offer them. This is possible if one spends disciplined time in the morning doing telephone calls to generate appointments. Maintaining discipline in this activity is most important.

The art of need analysis/need creation

A successful insurance advisor is always a master of need analyses. Need-based selling always increases customer satisfaction and leads to increased loyalty. Analysing the needs of clients is an art and follows a certain process:

- **Build rapport** – This is essential as it creates healthy interactions with the client. Some of the ways to build rapport are:
  - Be genuine

- ○ Listen actively
- ○ Empathise
- ○ Use positive body language
- ○ Find common ground
- **Ask the right questions** – This helps to understand the customer in depth. Generally, open-ended questions are best. When we ask the right questions, the exact needs of the customer come to light, and as an advisor, one can then provide the right solution. We need to focus on the customer's goals, while formulating questions and addressing their pain points. Summarising our understanding in front of the customer ensures no future misunderstanding of the identified needs.
- **Confirm the issue** – Before offering any solution, it is always important to confirm the customer's issues and concerns. This helps build confidence and conveys to the customer that, as an advisor, you can solve their issues, because you fully understand their situation.

Customising solutions promptly

When we meet clients, knowing their needs is of vital importance. Even if there is no obvious, visible need, we should be capable of creating one in the customer's mind. We have already established how to identify client needs, so the next step is to design tailored solutions for clients using all of the available products in our basket.

Some of the requirements to do this effectively include:

- **Product knowledge** – Advisors must clearly understand their products or solutions. This includes knowing which products suit which age groups, what life-stage needs they cater to, their features, and their benefits. This will help to combine products, in order to provide a comprehensive solution that satisfies all the possible needs of the customer.

- **Active listening** – Carefully listening to clients is crucial. Most times, customers provide hints about their requirements and expectations, including future or life-stage needs. Active listening makes it easier to design an effective solution.
- **Knowing the family** – When identifying needs, discussing the client's family members in detail is vital. This will allow you to offer specific products to specific family members, increasing the client's interest in investing.
- **Connecting the solution to the identified need** – It's critical to link the suggested solution to the multiple needs the customer has, or may have. Sometimes customers may not immediately understand why a particular solution is being provided. Connecting the solution to their needs multiple times during the discussion creates clarity and increases the likelihood of agreement. Advisors must check whether the customer has understood the solution during the conversation.

Agility in the post-sales approach

The most critical activity for any insurance advisor to remain consistent and successful over the years is to maintain a robust post-sales approach. Post-sales connections foster long-term trust with customers.

Closing a sale is just the first step; long-term success requires post-sales service. Key post-sales practices include:

- **First 100 days** – Advisors should visit new clients within the first 100 days for onboarding. This visit involves helping clients understand their policy documents, verifying their details (e.g., beneficiary nominee name, date of birth, and address, etc.), and clarifying any questions. Most importantly, the advisor should revisit the objective of the client's policy purchase.

- **100 days before the policy anniversary** – This phase ensures timely renewal payments and reassures the client of the advisor's reliability.
- **Building relationships** – Wishing clients on special occasions, festivals, and family milestones strengthens connections. Visiting clients during crises, staying updated on their events through social media, and connecting personally, all enhance trust.
- **Personalised approach** – Whenever possible, advisors should personally handle post-sales activities, as this undoubtedly deepens the connection.

Benefits of a strong post-sales approach:

- Good references
- Repeat sales from the same client
- Credibility through word-of-mouth recommendations

A great future in the insurance profession largely depends on the agility and consistency of an advisor's post-sales approach.

Continuous knowledge development as a financial advisor

To differentiate oneself in the highly competitive insurance profession, continuous knowledge enhancement is essential. Some ways to achieve this include:

- **Seeking mentorship** – Find a mentor to enhance your knowledge and skills.
- **Enrolling in courses** – Participate in online and offline courses offered by reputable institutions.
- **Attending webinars and seminars** – Join sessions conducted by industry experts, to gain insights.
- **Qualifying for MDRT and beyond** – Attend MDRT speaker sessions to foster growth, both personally and professionally.

Impact of knowledge development:

- Increased productivity and earnings
- Enhanced credibility in front of clients
- Clients see advisors as advanced, knowledgeable, and tech-savvy

Core practices for long-term success

Success in the insurance profession requires a disciplined, consistent approach. Essential practices include:

- **Good communication skills** – Focusing on both listening and speaking abilities.
- **Peer reviews** – Seeking feedback through mentor-mentee programmes.
- **Effective marketing** – Sharing views on social media to increase visibility.
- **Tracking progress** – Keeping records of meetings, calls, and appointments to identify areas for improvement.
- **Celebrating success** – Acknowledging achievements to build self-confidence.

Advisors should always prioritise clients' needs over personal earnings. Those who recommend the best products, regardless of commission, enjoy long-term success.

Key personality traits:

- **High energy levels** – Engaging with clients requires a consistently energetic approach.
- **Persistence** – Rejections are inevitable, but persistence leads to success.
- **Optimism** – Maintaining a positive outlook is crucial for growth.
- **Taking the initiative** – Success comes to those who act rather than wait.
- **Discipline** – Implementing learned skills, daily, differentiates successful advisors from the rest.

The importance of discipline

Maxwell Maltz, author of *Psycho-Cybernetics*, stated,

> *"The ability to discipline yourself to delay gratification in the short term, in order to enjoy greater rewards in the long term is the indispensable prerequisite for success."*

To succeed, advisors must adopt disciplined daily practices. The processes required in this profession may sometimes feel repetitive, but consistency leads to results.

Thomas Edison said it best:

> *"Our greatest weakness lies in giving up. The most certain way to succeed is always to try one more time."*

Failures are part of the journey, but they offer opportunities to learn and pivot towards success.

Conclusion

Understanding client behaviours and adapting to the changing dynamics of the insurance profession are crucial for long-term success. Advisors who focus on client needs, maintain discipline, and continually upgrade their skills, can thrive in this rewarding yet challenging field.

By following the core practices outlined in this chapter, financial advisors can overcome challenges, build meaningful client relationships, and achieve their professional and personal goals.

Chapter 6
The Art of Online Prospecting
Márta Borbála Király

Márta Borbála Király is a highly accomplished financial services professional with over a decade of experience in the profession. A member of the Million Dollar Round Table (MDRT) for eight years, she has earned four Top of the Table qualifications, a prestigious distinction that recognises the top 1% of financial advisors worldwide. Based in Hungary, Marta specialises in providing comprehensive financial planning to business owners, helping them navigate complex financial decisions and secure their financial futures.

Marta is also a dynamic speaker, known for sharing her practical ideas, which have piqued the curiosity of financial advisors from Miami to

Sydney. Her innovative approaches to financial planning have inspired many professionals worldwide to rethink their strategies and enhance their practices. Passionate about mentoring, Marta offers guidance and support to help the next generation of financial advisors grow and succeed.

Her commitment to excellence extends beyond her clients and colleagues, as she is an active supporter of the MDRT Foundation, dedicating her time and resources to charitable initiatives that make a positive impact on communities, globally.

Introduction

As the morning sun streamed through the large windows of his home office, John settled into his chair. The room was filled with the rich aroma of his morning coffee, and he had a sense of purpose. He wasn't just motivated—having clear goals of what he wanted to achieve—he also knew that to get where he wanted to be, he needed to do the magic technique in the financial profession.

As Henry David Thoreau said: *"Success usually comes to those who are too busy to be looking for it."*

The magic technique is **activity**.

He had two ways of ensuring effective activity:

1. Be happy with anyone who came across his path and became his client.
2. Decide who he wants to work with, or who he wants to come across his path during prospecting, in order to build a clientele with high-quality prospects.

He started by opening his calendar, but he faced an empty white space. While feeling uncertain, he asked himself:

"How will I fill these empty slots with qualified prospects?"

"How can I ensure that my days are filled with productive meetings?"

The question nagged at him: *"How do I fill my calendar effectively?"*

Have you as an advisor ever felt the same way? Have you dreamt about meeting as many prospects as possible, but were also faced with that *"white space"*.

In today's digital world, a real goldmine is social media, where you have the possibility to find an unlimited number of qualified prospects, but only if you do it the right way.

While sharing my experience about social media prospecting around the world, I have met three big myths about creating online content and prospecting that keep people from becoming successful:

Myth #1: "Finding HNW prospects is simply a numbers game"

It's not true. No, it's not a numbers game; the truth is it's a quality game. I'll soon explain what I mean by that.

Myth #2: "You need a lot of followers to jumpstart your business on social media"

Well, again, this is not true. You need a small group of devoted fans who come from your smallest viable market. You need followers from your target market. On some platforms, you don't even need followers to find good prospects. If you are interesting enough, a handful of people will do.

Myth #3: "You need to ask people about their network to get referrals"

To think like that is a big mistake! Instead of asking them, *"Who do you know?"* when I want to ask for referrals, I already know who they know. I point out the exact people I want to get in touch with. It's a different game, and it works.

In this chapter, I will show you three ways to jumpstart your business through social media prospecting. With these short tips, I guarantee that instead of a white space, you might even have *too many* meetings. Can you imagine that?

Now just picture that blank white page in your calendar. Imagine having a magic wand, and with each wave of the wand, you'll see your calendar filling up with meetings. Sounds exciting? Let's jump in! These tips are doable but work like magic every time.

LinkedIn prospecting

There are plenty of options for how you can find new prospects through LinkedIn. Let's start with a practical and easy-to-implement strategy, which can make asking for referrals easier. Some people still think that asking for referrals is no more than asking the question, *"Who do you know?"* but in my experience that won't give anyone good results. Instead, this strategy only delivers rejection and disappointment.

The trick with this technique is that instead of asking a client *"Who do you know?"*, you can already know who they know and who they are connected to, with the help of LinkedIn.

You will need to do some research before meeting a prospect for the first time. Map out the prospect's LinkedIn profile and see who the people are in their network that fit your target market and you would be happy to meet. On LinkedIn, you can find prospects who are CEOs, entrepreneurs, founders, or professionals. Make a list and ask the prospect the following:

> *"Dear prospect, there are people I would love to meet, and I saw on LinkedIn that they are in your network. How do you think it would be possible for me to meet them?"*

You will see that some people will offer their help at once and will introduce you to them, but if not, don't worry—you can still go on and make it easier for them:

> *"What can I do to make you feel comfortable about introducing me to this person?"*

Let's stop here for a moment. There is a reason behind this question and why I recommend that you ask it this way.

A few years ago, there was a study where 10,000 clients of financial advisors were asked what the reasons are why they don't give referrals. This is the largest study on the subject that I know of. It was found that one of the four main reasons is that even tough people, who might be happy to give referrals, don't know how to do it. They are unsure of how to make the introduction, if they should call the recommended people, or how to bring up a sensitive topic like finances.

This is why the second part of this script goes like this:

> *"Would you like to make a phone call, send an email, or use LinkedIn; should I come to your office, or would you like us have a coffee together, etc.? Of course, if you wish, I can give you some tips on what usually works and what you could say to them."*

There is a psychological theory called the self-determination theory (SDT), developed by psychologists Edward Deci and Richard Ryan in the 1980s. SDT says that autonomy is one of the fundamental human psychological needs. When people feel they have control over their actions and decisions, their intrinsic motivation increases. This theory emphasises that providing choices enhances individuals' sense of autonomy, leading to higher engagement and persistence in tasks.

This means that **choice is a motivation**. By asking them what would make them feel comfortable, you give them the freedom of choice, which raises the probability that they will actually help you.

I recommend offering between five and ten names, so that there's a bigger chance you'll come up with people they know well.

Another way to use this approach is when you build your network or create new connections that fit your ideal client profile. You can check who the people are that you both know. Once you know that, you might be just one introduction away from a prospect you would like to meet.

Now it is time to take hold of your magic wand again. Let's give it a wave—I'll show you what to do next to feed even more appointments onto that calendar page.

Facebook prospecting

If you want terrific results from Facebook prospecting while only spending a reasonable amount of money, I'd like to share a three-step formula with you.

> *Facebook is a café full of people. Your only job is to invite them to your table.*

You will get terrific results by inviting the right people. Just as in real life, you don't want everyone to sit down at your table. You want to use your time to its highest and best use. Prospecting is about separating people into two groups: **target** and **non-target**.

Often, you'll hear people share negative opinions about this space: *"You can't meet wealthy people through Facebook prospecting; the wealthy stay off social media sites."*

For those who don't have a plan, these can, unfortunately, be valid points. How can it be then that I've connected with celebrities, actresses, and high-net-worth individuals on Facebook since the pandemic began?

Facebook prospecting sounds exciting and easy. In truth, it's exciting, but it's not easy. Proximity doesn't guarantee interest or curiosity. Even if you're in the same room with someone, it still takes a well-executed plan to achieve the desired result.

Many financial advisors have advertised on Facebook. I have too, but my hit rate is many times higher. Why? Because I have a plan, and that is: **Attract, Know the process, and Close the sale**.

When you post, you'll need to do so in a way that communicates to your target that they have an issue regarding their financial future—and you are the advisor with the experience and knowledge needed to solve the issue.

Márta Borbála Király

It would be counterproductive if all you did was make your prospect aware of the challenge facing them, and then have the prospect turn to someone else for help. You must simultaneously educate your future client about their issue and your ability to solve it. You are the guru.

I advise you to work with a professional marketing strategist and use the three-step **pinwheel formula**. The pinwheel symbolises the focused energy of channelling the attention of your target market.

The three steps are as follows:

1. **Attract**

What topic or product do you have that offers a unique feature for the client? Writing good ads is not easy—I highly recommend working with a professional.

You need to find a good balance between generating strong feelings in your audience and positioning yourself as the source of the solution (without violating Facebook's rules).

Be specific with your message. My content speaks to a previously defined target market, who are business owners. I have been working with the SME market for more than 10 years and it gives me a great opportunity to work with quality clients, even with the help of the Face-book Ads tool.

What do I mean by being specific?

For example:

- Don't run a generic ad about pension plans. Instead, run an ad about **pension planning for business owners**.

- Don't simply run an ad about life insurance. Run an ad about **shareholder protection.**

More tips to help you be more effective:

- You will also want to be engaging with your Facebook Ad. You need to raise people's attention. A great way of doing that is to start with a strong question. For example: *Do you want to thrive or barely survive after retirement?*
- Using stories in your ads can also be attractive. You could write about critical illness generally, or you could tell the story of a father who suffered from a critical illness and left his family in desperate financial circumstances.

2. **Know the process**

Let's assume your activity on Facebook produces results. Your prospect responds to a specific topic. The prospect will very likely ask you to send them the terms and prices in an email. If you meet a prospect following an introduction from a client, this won't happen.

Version A:

a. The lead arrives.
b. You call the prospect, who enquires about the topic in more detail; you speak about the topic for 5 to 10 minutes.
c. You get excited, because the prospect asks for an offer, which you send immediately.
d. Two days pass and you call the prospect to set up a meeting.
e. All that is left is to sign the contract.

The problem with this approach is that it almost never works. Why? The same reason it doesn't work with a cold call or introduction. You haven't established trust with the prospect. You end up in a situation where the prospect will 'forget' to answer your calls.

How do you avoid this? Whether online or in person, your presence is needed, in order to succeed. In a normal sales process, you need to manage the flow. This doesn't mean you send an offer after a ten-minute chat. The offer will likely never be read or understood.

The correct process:

a. The lead arrives.
b. Within 24 hours you call the prospect and position yourself by showing a vision of what it's like to work with you. While you are doing this, you are also qualifying the prospect to ensure that they found who they were looking for and that you also found your target prospect. It's easiest to do this by asking questions to see what they already know about your topic. You can fill in the missing gaps. Don't ask for an appointment immediately. Use the qualifying questions to build trust. During the call, we can subtly ask for a lead using the following question: *"Is the protective product only for him or is it interesting for the whole family?"*
c. Only after the above steps can you ask for an appointment. When someone contacts you electronically, it is usually easy to schedule an online meeting with them. 80-90% of 'Facebook meetings' happen online. During this meeting, we can make another mistake by immediately preparing a calculation for the client. My experience is it's better to share any offer or calculation at a future meeting, allowing more time to build mutual trust. After we have fine-tuned the calculations with the client, then we can email the offer.

Let's assume your activity on Facebook produces results and your prospects respond to a specific topic. If you haven't established trust, however, your leads might go cold.

The correct process includes:

- calling the prospect promptly to position yourself, build trust, and qualify the lead.
- scheduling an online or in-person meeting where you can further refine the conversation.
- only presenting tailored solutions after trust has been established.

3. **Close the sale**

Once you've attracted the right people and followed the proper process, all that remains is closing the sale during your meeting.

Having attracted the right people and followed the right process, there is nothing more left to do, other than a personal meeting to close the sale.

Facebook prospecting is an exciting and powerful tool to help grow your business. It's crowded and loud, and you need to get the right target sitting at your table in the café. If you use the right process after the lead arrives, you increase your chances of closing the deal dramatically. Once you do it well, I promise that you and your clients will prepare some of the most delicious meals together for many years to come. And that's something to look forward to. Bon appétit!

And now for the final wave of our magic wand to fill up those calendar pages to the fullest. I hope you start feeling the self-confidence of a mighty prospecting wizard!

Webinars

A dynamic approach to generating immediate sales through webinars is the "Jolly Joker" strategy. Why "Jolly Joker"? Because it's your chance to deliver a powerful message, entertain your audience, and seal the deal—all in one go.

Imagine a virtual space where you can invite anyone you want without worrying about guest compatibility. You have the freedom to choose from a variety of engaging topics that resonate with your target market. At the same time, you don't need to spend 90 minutes with each participant sharing your expertise. Instead, you can speak to many people at once.

Who can you invite to your webinar?

My answer is simple: everyone! Webinars are a powerhouse for your prospecting efforts. You can bring together existing clients, friends, past leads who said no before, and your centres of influence.

Webinars work if you create a topic that resonates with your target market. My target market is business owners, so let me share a simple but powerful way of attracting them.

Imagine a tailored opportunity where business owners can delve into complex topics in a concise, informative manner. At our 30-minute Zoom webinars, we aim to provide a sneak peek—a "meeting before the first meeting" if you will—into key subjects that can significantly impact both your and their business strategies. These are pre-meeting webinars.

Why pre-meeting webinars?

- **Efficiency:** Time is highly valuable for business owners. Instead of committing to lengthy initial meetings, concise sessions offer a snapshot of critical topics.
- **Engagement:** By keeping it short and focused, you ensure that business owners get a taste of what each topic entails without overwhelming them with details upfront.
- **Decision-making:** At the end of each webinar, participants have the opportunity to ask questions and assess which topics resonate most with their current needs and challenges.

The following topics are covered:

1. Protection for business owners
2. Retirement planning for business owners
3. Strategic capital surplus
4. Employee loyalty programmes (supporting the new generation in the business and supporting exit strategies)
5. Shareholder protection
6. Legacy planning

Following the webinar, business owners who express interest in specific topics proceed to a personalised first meeting online. This approach ensures that subsequent discussions are focused, informed, and aligned with their business goals.

The pre-meeting webinars are designed to bridge the gap between exploration and action. They offer a glimpse into transformative topics, empowering business owners to make informed decisions efficiently.

This is, of course, just one example. You can also offer webinars on retirement planning for business owners. Once you know your audience well enough, you can tailor the topics to meet their needs.

Conclusion

In this chapter, I've shown you four ways to jumpstart your business through social media prospecting:

- LinkedIn prospecting
- Practical strategies for Facebook prospecting
- Webinars
- Understanding the psychology behind referrals

John, from the start of our chapter, was very satisfied after implementing these ideas. These strategies transformed that scary "white space" into a bustling schedule full of productive meetings. Imagine having too many meetings to handle!

With tools like LinkedIn and Facebook, and a strategic approach to webinars, you now have a comprehensive toolkit. Implement these strategies, and watch as your calendar fills up with quality prospects and meaningful appointments.

Remember, in the digital age, a strategic approach to social media can unlock doors you never thought possible. So go ahead, turn that white space into gold, and embrace the opportunities that lie ahead. Your journey to success is just a few clicks away.

Now that we're done with this journey and you're full of ideas, I know what you're thinking. The one question I always get from my audience in every conference room, in every corner of the globe, is this: *"Okay, Marti, but where should I start?"*

The answer is simple, though I know it's not easy to put into practice: **Find the target market that you would really like to serve.**

Our profession is about service, and you have to love the people you choose to serve as an advisor. Only then will you be able to enjoy what you do.

Part Three

Branding and Marketing

Chapter 7
Brand Mastery - Crafting and Elevating Your Advisor Identity
Kobus Kleyn

Kobus Kleyn is an accomplished author and thought leader in financial planning, with decades of experience as a Certified Financial Planner®, tax practitioner, and fiduciary practitioner. He holds postgraduate qualifications in financial planning from the University of Free State, and an MDP & AEP from UNISA, along with designations from FPI, SAIT, FISA, and STEP.

Globally recognised, Kobus is a lifetime MDRT member and a founding member of the Global Life Happens Ambassadors team, advocating for financial literacy and awareness. He has authored over 200 articles and six books, including *Passion for the Profession* and *From Burnout to Bliss*, which reflects on self-care in the financial services profession.

Kobus Kleyn

Kobus's work continues to elevate the financial planning profession, inspiring professionals and clients to achieve success. His dedication to excellence and innovation has set a benchmark for others in the field. By sharing his insights and experiences, he empowers individuals to embrace financial planning as a tool for achieving lasting fulfilment.

Introduction

The financial advisory profession is fiercely competitive, with countless professionals vying for the attention and trust of prospective clients. In such an environment, establishing a distinctive personal brand is not merely an advantage but a fundamental necessity for survival and success. This differentiation is crucial for financial advisors seeking to stand out in a sea of similarity, where many offer services that, on the surface, appear interchangeable.

A personal brand serves as a beacon, guiding clients through the crowded marketplace to the advisor whose values, approach, and expertise resonate most closely with their financial aspirations and needs. This branding goes beyond the mere listing of services offered; it encompasses the advisor's entire persona, from their approach to financial planning and investment strategies to how they communicate and build relationships with clients.

Simon Sinek's insight, *"People don't buy what you do; they buy why you do it,"* underscores the profound impact of a personal brand. Clients are drawn to advisors who provide financial advice and share a compelling narrative about why they do what they do. This narrative can stem from personal experiences, a unique approach to financial management, or a deep-seated belief in helping clients achieve their financial dreams. It's the 'why' behind an advisor's work that establishes a deep connection with clients, fostering trust and loyalty.

In a practical sense, a strong personal brand lets financial advisors articulate their unique value proposition clearly. This combination of personal and professional qualities sets an advisor apart. It could be an unparalleled understanding of a specific market sector, a unique approach to risk management, or a particularly empathetic client service model. Whatever the elements of this value proposition, they must be communicated consistently across all platforms and interactions, from the advisor's website and social media presence to their speaking engagements and published content.

Furthermore, brand differentiation in financial advising extends to the advisor's ability to encapsulate their expertise and approach into a compelling story. This narrative should weave together the advisor's professional qualifications, experiences, and successes with their journey and motivations. It's about creating a brand that feels authentic and relatable, not just to any client, but specifically to the kind of client the advisor is most passionate about serving.

By effectively communicating a unique personal brand, financial advisors can attract clients with similar values and financial goals, establishing a foundation for a fruitful, long-lasting professional relationship. This alignment not only makes for more satisfying client interactions but also enhances the advisor's ability to tailor their services to their clientele's specific needs and preferences.

Trust and Relationship Building

With financial planning, trust is not just a commodity but the currency of success. The essence of this trust transcends the conventional advisor-client dynamic, elevating it to a partnership rooted in deep understanding and mutual respect. This is where a well-defined personal brand becomes instrumental. A personal brand is more than a mere marketing tool—it is a beacon of trustworthiness, signalling an advisor's dedication to their client's financial prosperity.

For clients, entrusting someone with their financial future is a significant leap of faith. They are investing not only their resources but also their hopes, dreams, and their families' financial security. In this context, a personal brand acts as a bridge, narrowing the gap between uncertainty and confidence. It allows clients to see beyond the advisor's professional facade, offering a glimpse into their ethos, values, and genuine commitment to safeguarding their client's financial well-being.

A compelling personal brand showcases an advisor's unique approach to financial management—not as a one-size-fits-all solution but as a tailored strategy reflecting a deep understanding of the client's individual goals, challenges, and aspirations. This bespoke approach, underpinned by the advisor's distinct values and expertise, fosters a sense of familiarity and trust.

Research by Edelman, a renowned global communications firm, underscores the critical role of trust in the advisor-client relationship. Their findings reveal that trust eclipses other factors, such as performance and reputation, when clients choose a financial advisor. This underscores the essential nature of trust in building and sustaining professional relationships within the financial advisory sector.

Identifying your Unique Brand Identity: Self-Reflection and Authenticity

Embarking on the journey to define a personal brand requires a thorough exploration of the essence of who you are as a professional and, more importantly, as a person. This introspective process involves a candid assessment of one's core values, beliefs, and the unique blend of experiences and skills that one brings to the table. It's about uncovering and articulating the authentic self in a way that resonates with your intended audience.

Authenticity is the cornerstone of a powerful personal brand. It ensures that the brand is not just a façade or a series of marketing tactics but an accurate representation of the advisor's personality, values, and professional approach. This authenticity builds credibility and relatability, enabling clients to connect with the advisor more personally.

Questions for reflection are pivotal in this process. Advisors should ponder their motivations, vision for their clients' financial futures, and the impact they wish to make in their professional realm. *What drives you? What do you stand for? How do your personal experiences shape your approach to financial advising?* These questions are not merely rhetorical but foundational pillars upon which a genuine and compelling personal brand is built.

Echoing Oscar Wilde's wisdom, *"Be yourself; everyone else is already taken,"* the pursuit of authenticity is not just advisable but essential. In a world where clients are bombarded with generic marketing messages and impersonal service offerings, a personal brand grounded in authenticity stands out. It speaks to the heart of what clients are truly seeking: a financial advisor who is not just a service provider but a trusted partner, advisor, and ally on their financial journey.

By intertwining the principles of trust, relationship building, and authenticity, financial advisors can craft personal brands that differentiate them in a crowded market and foster deep, enduring connections with their clients. These connections, built on a solid foundation of trust and mutual respect, are the lifeblood of a successful financial advisory practice.

Building a Brand Strategy: Key Components and Objectives

Crafting a coherent and compelling brand strategy is akin to setting the sails for a journey across the vast ocean of the financial advising market. It requires meticulous planning, keen insight, and a deep understanding of your strengths and your target audience's needs. A successful brand strategy is built on several foundational pillars that, when combined, steer your brand towards achieving its full potential.

Defining Clear Objectives Aligned with Business Goals

The first step in building your brand strategy is to define clear, measurable objectives that align with your overarching business goals. These objectives serve as beacons, guiding your branding efforts and ensuring they contribute directly to your business's growth and success. Objectives might range from increasing your visibility in the market to attracting a specific demographic of clients, enhancing client retention rates, or scaling your business operations.

These objectives must be SMART: specific, measurable, achievable, relevant, and time-bound. For example, instead of a vague goal like "increase brand awareness," a SMART objective would be to *"increase website traffic by 20% within the next six months through targeted social media campaigns."*

Understanding the Target Audience

A profound understanding of your target audience is the cornerstone of any successful brand strategy. Knowing who your ideal clients are— understanding their needs, challenges, preferences, and financial goals —enables you to tailor your brand messaging to resonate with them on a personal level.

This entails conducting market research to gather insights into your audience's demographics, psychographics, and behaviour. Surveys, interviews, and online behaviour analyses can provide valuable information about what your target clients value, the channels they frequent, and the type of content that engages them. This understanding allows you to position your brand as the answer to their specific financial questions and needs.

Positioning Yourself Uniquely in the Market

With a clear set of objectives and a deep understanding of your target audience, the next step is positioning your brand uniquely in the marketplace. This involves distinguishing yourself from competitors by highlighting what makes you different and better suited to meet their needs.

Unique positioning can be based on various factors, such as your specific expertise in a niche area of financial advising, your approach to financial planning and management, your use of technology, or even your personality and values as they relate to your business practice. For example, if you specialise in retirement planning for high-net-worth individuals, your brand should reflect the sophistication, expertise, and personalised service this audience expects.

Establishing Thought Leadership

Many financial advisors' significant objective is to establish themselves as thought leaders within a specific domain of financial advising. Thought leadership is a powerful component of a brand strategy, as it demonstrates expertise, enhances credibility, and builds trust with your audience.

Kobus Kleyn

Establishing thought leadership involves creating and sharing valuable content that addresses the interests and challenges of your target audience, participating in discussions, and contributing to professional forums and publications. By consistently providing insights and valuable advice, you position yourself as an authority in your profession, attracting more clients and opportunities for professional growth.

Audience Targeting and Positioning

In financial advising, audience targeting and positioning is akin to navigating a complex maze. Each turn represents decisions and strategies that lead you closer to your ideal clients—those whose needs and aspirations align perfectly with your services. Understanding your target audience is not just crucial; it is the foundation of successful brand positioning.

Who are your Ideal Clients?

Identifying your ideal clients involves going beyond basic demographics to delve into your audience's psychographics—understanding their behaviours, values, lifestyles, and financial aspirations. Are they young professionals at the outset of their wealth-building journey, or are they nearing retirement and looking for strategies to protect their nest egg? Perhaps they are entrepreneurs seeking advice on business growth and asset protection.

Each market segment has distinct financial goals, challenges, and preferences. By identifying these, advisors can tailor their messaging, services, and value propositions to speak directly to the needs of their specific audience.

Understanding Financial Goals and Challenges

Once you have a clear picture of your ideal clients, the next step is to gain a deep understanding of their financial goals and the challenges they face in achieving those goals. This involves asking questions, conducting surveys, or engaging in one-on-one conversations.

For instance, young professionals might be focused on debt management and saving for a first home, while high-net-worth individuals could be more concerned with wealth preservation and tax planning. Entrepreneurs might need advice on cash flow management and business expansion. By understanding these goals and challenges, you can position your brand as the go-to source for solutions in these areas.

Meeting the Needs and Preferences of your Target Clients

Understanding your clients' preferences in receiving and interacting with financial advice is equally important. Some clients may prefer in-depth, face-to-face consultations, while others might appreciate the convenience of digital platforms offering tools and resources for financial planning. Tailoring your service delivery and communication channels to match these preferences is crucial in positioning your brand effectively.

Moreover, your brand messaging should resonate with the values and aspirations of your target audience. For example, if your target clients highly value transparency and ethical investing, these principles should be prominently reflected in your brand's messaging and service offerings.

Seth Godin's Wisdom: Focus on the people who want what you've got

Seth Godin's advice, *"Don't try to please everyone. There are countless people who don't want what you've got. Focus on the people who do,"* is particularly pertinent here. It's tempting to cast a wide net to attract more clients, but a more focused approach is often more effective. You can build stronger, more meaningful relationships with your clients by targeting a specific market segment, and positioning your brand to meet their unique needs.

This focused approach also allows you to become an expert in addressing the specific challenges and opportunities your target audience faces. It sets you apart from competitors who may take a more generalised approach, enhancing your brand's value proposition.

Implementing your Branding Through Multiple Channels: Digital and Traditional Methods

Building and maintaining a dynamic online presence is indispensable for financial advisors in today's interconnected world. The digital landscape offers a plethora of platforms for advisors to showcase their expertise, connect with clients, and differentiate themselves from the competition. However, branding extends beyond the digital domain, intertwining traditional methods with modern strategies to create a holistic approach to brand promotion and communication.

Digital Branding: Harnessing the Power of Online Platforms

- **LinkedIn:** As a professional networking site, LinkedIn is invaluable for establishing your professional identity, sharing insights, and connecting with peers and potential clients.

Regular posts, articles, and active participation in relevant groups can position you as a thought leader in your profession.

- **Professional blogs:** A well-maintained blog is a platform for sharing in-depth knowledge, offering financial advice, and discussing current trends in our profession. It's a tool for demonstrating expertise and adding a personal touch to your brand, showcasing your unique perspective on financial planning and investment strategies.
- **Personal websites:** Your website acts as the digital storefront of your brand, offering a comprehensive overview of your services, values, and professional ethos. Incorporating client testimonials, case studies, and a regularly updated blog can enhance credibility and engage visitors.
- **Social media:** Platforms such as LinkedIn, X, Facebook, TikTok, and Instagram allow for more informal interactions with clients and prospects. They can be used to share quick tips, company news, and insights into your professional life, thereby humanising your brand and building a community around it.

Traditional Branding: The Timeless Value of Personal Connections

- **Introductions:** In financial advising, word-of-mouth endorsement remains one of the most potent tools for client acquisition. Encouraging satisfied clients to introduce friends and family can significantly boost your clientele and enhance your brand's reputation.
- **Networking events:** Attending conferences, seminars, and local business events provides opportunities to meet potential

clients face-to-face, expand your professional network, and establish your presence in the financial community.

- **Print media:** While digital media dominates much of today's marketing, traditional print media such as brochures, business cards, and newsletters can still play a crucial role, especially when targeting demographics less inclined towards digital consumption.

Balancing Digital and Traditional Methods

The synergy between digital and traditional branding methods allows financial advisors to maximise their reach and impact. While digital strategies offer scalability and access to a broad audience, traditional methods provide a personal touch and foster deeper connections.

Emphasising Gary Vaynerchuk's sentiment, *"The best marketing strategy ever: care,"* underscores the importance of genuine engagement and empathy in all branding efforts. Whether through a thoughtful blog post, a personalised email newsletter, or a one-on-one meeting at a networking event, showing that you care about your clients' financial well-being is paramount.

Measuring the Success of your Personal Branding Strategy: Metrics and Tools

In the digital age, the effectiveness of a personal branding strategy is not left to intuition or guesswork. Specific metrics and analytical tools offer a quantifiable glimpse into the success of your branding efforts, enabling adjustments and strategic pivots to enhance brand impact and reach.

Online Presence

- **Measuring online visibility:** Tools like Google Search Console provide insights into website performance, search engine optimisation (SEO), and content rankings.
- **Improving online presence:** Enhance visibility by focusing on SEO best practices, regularly updating your website with high-quality content, and maintaining active social media profiles.

Engagement

- **Tracking audience interaction:** Engagement metrics such as likes, comments, shares, and mentions on social media, as well as website metrics like page views and 'time on page', provide valuable insights.
- **Boosting engagement:** Tailor content to your audience's interests, and encourage participation through polls, questions, and calls to action.

Conversions

- **Measuring goal achievement:** Tools like Google Analytics track lead generation, newsletter signups, service inquiries, and sales.
- **Enhancing conversions:** Optimise calls to action, and ensure messaging clearly articulates value propositions.

Conclusion

Creating and nurturing a personal brand in financial advising is both an art and a science. It demands authenticity, strategic acumen, and a deep commitment to meaningfully engaging with clients and the community. By leveraging a mix of digital and traditional branding methods, financial advisors can carve out a unique space in a crowded marketplace that resonates with their target audience and reflects their professional ethos and personal values.

The meticulous measurement of branding efforts ensures that the personal brand you build not only stands the test of time but also becomes a beacon for those seeking guidance in the complex world of financial planning and investment.

Chapter 8
From Wow to Aha
Priti Kucheria

Priti Kucheria, CFP®, LUTCF, hails from India and is a 24-year MDRT member with two Court of the Table and 21 Top of the Table honours. She is the founding principal of Kucheria Financial Services, a family office offering comprehensive financial services under one roof.

She has consistently been the top producer at her company, earning accolades for highest persistency, highest assets under management, highest sum assured, highest online selling, and more. Over the years, Priti has served on several MDRT committees, including as a Global Council Member and an MDRT Brand Ambassador, where she has played a pivotal role in shaping the future of the profession.

As an inspiring speaker, Priti has addressed audiences in various countries, motivating advisors to achieve exceptional results. Her clients praise her professionalism and the seamless, personalised service they receive from her and her team. Priti believes in building lifelong relationships, ensuring that every client interaction is both meaningful and impactful.

Priti's commitment to empowering women in finance has been a hallmark of her career. She actively mentors aspiring female advisors, encouraging them to break barriers and excel in a traditionally male-dominated profession. Her dedication to creating a positive and inclusive work culture has earned her the respect and admiration of peers and clients alike.

Introduction

In the fast-paced world of financial advising, a select group stands out —the MDRTians. They belong to the elite Million Dollar Round Table association and are the crème de la crème of the profession. Their dedication and hard work have propelled them to the top 1% in the world, earning them the accolades and respect they rightfully deserve.

What sets them apart in their journey to this point in their career has been their dedication, perseverance, and pursuit of excellence. The sense of achievement and pride in becoming part of this exclusive club is undeniable. I refer to them as 'wow' advisors. However, this is not the destination. It is essential to pause, reflect, and ask the inevitable question: What's the next milestone?

From Satisfaction to Delight

How does one stand out in a competitive world filled with accomplished financial advisors? The answer lies in taking client satisfaction to another level. It involves evolving oneself from a "wow" advisor to an "aha" one—from "good" to the "best in class". Customer acquisition and engagement processes must flow into retention, re-acquisition, and auto-replication.

The success of any business strategy hinges on the satisfaction of its clients. No one in the financial advisory profession intentionally wants their clients to leave unsatisfied with a bad taste in their mouths. The goal, however, is to ensure that they don't leave you feeling satisfied— they need to feel delighted. This is the key to fostering consistently paced growth as clients transform from satisfied to loyal.

In the ever-evolving business landscape, products and services are no longer the sole competitive differentiators for financial advisors. Businesses increasingly recognise that it is not just about what you offer but how you offer it. The focus has shifted towards the experience that clients receive throughout their journey—transitioning from good customer service to extraordinary client experiences.

Good service is simply the starting point; phenomenal experiences become the cornerstone of enduring relationships. They are the recipe for long-term success in this profession.

Creating Phenomenal Client Experiences

Good service might earn you a place in your clients' short-term memories, but a phenomenal experience becomes etched in their hearts. It is the shift from a customer saying,

> *"Wow, I think I'll buy from him/her again,"* to, *"Aha! I have finally found the right one. I'm never going anywhere else."*

Instead of the client being a source of reference, you become inherently referable. In the "wow" state, you might receive references when you ask for them, but in the "aha" state, your clients are not just willing to introduce you to their family, friends, and associates, they are eager to do so. They almost want to show you off!

The ability to become referable is a testament to the exceptional experience you provide to your clients. It is no longer about making a sale but creating lasting relationships. When your clients have "aha" moments during their interactions with you, you become their champion, and they become your promoters.

They are not just satisfied; they are enchanted by the service and care you provide. Your presence in their life is a source of joy and security. What follows is a continuous and consistent thread of introductions that can multiply exponentially if you do it right every single time. They will ensure that your reputation as *'the trusted one'* precedes you.

Turning Insights into Actionable Plans

Clients have come to expect a personalised and memorable experience. The transition from "wow" to "aha" is not just a choice but a necessity, in order to stay relevant in the current market. It is a journey that demands a profound understanding of not just your client's needs and wants but their dreams and desires, likes and dislikes, hopes and aspirations, and much more.

The secret to reaching the zenith of this profession begins with a simple yet critical mantra: making a paradigm shift from meeting your client's expectations to exceeding them—at every touchpoint. This can happen by mastering the art of personalisation. The following are our practices, which can be personalised at various stages, allowing you to compare the difference that the client would experience when working with an ordinary "wow" advisor versus an extraordinary "aha" one.

First Interaction

No interaction can be merely transactional, especially the first one. First impressions are often the most enduring ones. When clients visit your office, making it a memorable experience, from before they arrive to after they leave, is essential.

- **Pre-arrival**: Reconfirm the appointment a day prior, sending the location and a landmark so they don't waste even a minute figuring out how to get there. Share a picture of the façade of the building. Consider hiring a valet service to ensure they don't have to worry about parking.
- **Arrival**: As they enter your office, create a warm and inviting ambience with well-lit spaces, pleasant surroundings, soothing sounds like flowing water and birds twittering, and a refreshing scent.
- **Greeting**: As your client enters the conference room, a personalised greeting on the screen adds a personal touch. You can further set the tone by playing an introductory film that introduces them to your team and the bandwidth of services you offer.
- **Beverage preferences**: Record their beverage preferences and have the staff ready with them at every other meeting thereafter. As the meeting concludes, accompany them to the elevator lobby with a team member.

Small and simple gestures like these go a long way in making your clients feel important and valued. They enhance the experience and significantly impact how they will perceive you.

Fact Finding

"Wow" advisors are straightforward in their dealings. They address the client's immediate insurance needs and provide information on available policies and their costs. Extraordinary advisors, however, will start with an in-depth consultation to understand the client's goals (other than the financial ones), lifestyle, preferences, past experiences (good and bad), apprehensions and fears, the reason why they have approached you, and more—thereby laying the foundation for tailored recommendations.

As an "aha" financial advisor, you must go beyond the ordinary. For example, instead of merely noting birth dates, invest time understanding how clients celebrate special occasions for various family members.

I remember a client being eternally grateful on his daughter's birthday when the balloon guy didn't turn up, and we could provide one at the last moment. Relentlessly gather data and develop creative ways to add value and deliver "aha" moments based on the insights you gain.

Ask open-ended questions to dig and discover what truly matters to them in connection with their goals, priorities, and concerns, and then actively listen so that you can weave it into solutions. For example, a "wow" advisor might focus solely on figures to arrive at a retirement corpus. An "aha" advisor would first ask what retirement means to the client. Have they experienced living with an elderly person? Who do they think they could depend on if a health issue rendered them entirely dependent?

You'll be surprised at the kind of stories that emerge, giving you that one opportunity to create an "aha" moment. One client had the money to take care of an aunt he held in high regard but couldn't find a suitable caretaker. We interviewed several candidates through our house help agency and provided one within a week. The lady blessed us, and our relationship with the client became permanently bonded.

We were confident about delivering a good retirement plan for him, but such value-added actions elevated the relationship to another level.

Solutions

Although you constantly guide your clients, stay committed to continuously educating yourself. Keep updated on industry trends, market conditions, and regulations, and exchange knowledge with your peers. There is much to learn from one another. Share relevant information with your prospects and clients to keep them abreast of potential opportunities and challenges.

This not only illustrates your professionalism but also shows that you care.

Take the initiative to educate your clients, not just about products or competitive financial instruments, but also about insurance and financial concepts, associated risks, investment strategies, and more. Provide clear and simple explanations with visual graphics to empower them to make informed decisions.

Tailor recommendations to fit the unique circumstances of each client. Avoid the one-size-fits-all approach and be prepared to explain the reasoning behind your recommendations. Conduct a thorough assessment and comprehensively analyse your client's current financial situation. Establish a financial safety net to navigate unexpected financial challenges. Discuss and integrate estate planning into your client's financial plans. Help them plan the transfer of assets through wills, trusts, powers of attorney, nominations, and beneficiaries.

Plan Execution

Execute all paperwork for the client as seamlessly and conveniently as possible. Request all documents in one go, and not piecemeal. When obtaining signatures on documents where a meeting is not required, send your representative to the client's office or home. For clients from out of town, go the extra mile to cover the cost of the return courier. Such gestures demonstrate your dedication to their satisfaction.

When a trip to the registrar's office is necessary, anticipate every detail. Provide a black ink pen, a stamp pad for fingerprints, wet wipes, and anything else that could make the process smooth and efficient.

During medicals, don't just accompany the clients to the lab; stay with them for the process and enjoy breakfast together afterwards.

For select clients, arrange chauffeur pick-up and drop-off services. This elevates their experience with you and demonstrates your commitment to their convenience and comfort.

Accessibility

You must maintain a high level of accessibility to attend to any query at any point in time. After working hours, or when you are unavailable, for whatever reason, ensure that clients are informed about your next availability, or the contact person they can deal with in your absence, through automatic voice messages, return emails, and so on.

Return missed calls promptly, and make sure that the turnaround time for your response to their emails becomes part of your unique identity. Typically, it should not be more than 24 hours.

When you update the client's policy and assets under management, anticipate the clarifications they may seek and be ready to address them promptly.

Offer as many communication channels and platforms as possible, besides the usual phone and email, such as Zoom, Teams, Skype, WhatsApp, Botim, Telegram, and chatbots. However, always prioritise face-to-face meetings when necessary and possible; don't settle for a phone call when personal interaction adds value.

Utilise technology to make the journey convenient for your clients. This could include digital policy access and their entire portfolio or mobile apps for managing policies. Install financial planning software and digital tools to easily access financial information and track progress towards goals.

Communication

Clear, open, and proactive communication is essential.

- **Onboarding**: After onboarding a client, inform them of the policy issuance before they hear from the company. Send a thank-you email, welcoming them as valued clients. Inform them about the free look period available, which allows them to review their policy.
- **Empathy**: Show empathy and sensitivity, especially in difficult situations such as claims relating to accidents, illnesses, or losses.
- **Network connections**: When needed, connect clients with other professionals in your network, such as tax advisors or estate planning attorneys.
- **Personal touch**: Personalise birthday and holiday greetings. Have every staff member who has interacted with the client

sign the cards. It's a tangible way of showing that your entire team values the client.

Service

Be responsive and prompt in your service.

- **Promises**: Make promises to your clients and stick to them. But don't stop there—strive to deliver more than they expected. For instance, if a client has a family member expecting a baby, offer guidance on procuring a birth certificate or adding the newborn to their health plan before they even think about it. Always under-promise and over-deliver.
- **Claims**: Offer guidance and help with the paperwork during the claim process. Make the entire experience hassle-free, and expedite the payout. More importantly, offer your availability for any assistance they may need. Your support during these times will make a positive, lasting impression.
- **Value-added services**: Go the extra mile, offering value-added services like regular policy reviews to ensure their coverage remains aligned with goals and risk tolerance. Rebalance portfolios when necessary. Keep them informed about changes in the insurance landscape and opportunities for improvement or cost savings.
- **Feedback**: Seek feedback from your clients on your services and actively work on improving your offerings based on their input.

Team Training

The "aha" culture cannot be limited to yourself. It must permeate every individual in your staff. It's about creating an ethos within your team dedicated to exceeding client expectations.

Team members should be trained to pay attention to detail, understand the importance of personalisation, and constantly be on the lookout for creating exceptional experiences. Create a system whereby no detail or process is overlooked or missed.

Share success stories, recognise and reward exceptional service, and provide ongoing training and feedback to foster continuous improvement. Encourage your team to embrace a culture of excellence.

Conclusion

The path to enduring success lies in not only your financial acumen but also the everlasting impression you leave on those you serve. It forms the basis of the shift from "wow" to "aha." It is an ongoing commitment to creating exceptional client experiences. It's about making every interaction count, surprising and delighting your clients at every turn, and ultimately traversing the journey from impressing your clients to making them your brand evangelists.

By consistently delivering excellence in all areas, you can build solid and long-lasting relationships with your clients as their trusted insurance and financial advisor. This would result in a long pipeline of quality prospects introduced by satisfied and enchanted clients. They not only remain loyal but become advocates for your services.

This kind of word-of-mouth marketing is powerful as it is a testament to the exceptional experiences you provide.

Priti Kucheria

As you embark on this journey, remember that each "aha" moment is a step toward becoming the "best in class" financial advisor and, ultimately, a trusted partner in your client's financial success. Consequently, it will catapult you from MDRT to COT and ultimately to TOT, making you a true luminary.

Chapter 9
The Power of Storytelling in Shaping Professional Success
Rima Antonios

Rima Antonios is a seasoned insurance consultant and financial advisor with over 25 years of experience at MetLife. Her career is dedicated to empowering individuals and businesses with tailored financial solutions that address their unique insurance and investment needs.

Antonios specialises in crafting life insurance packages designed to secure her clients' short- and long-term goals. Whether planning for educational needs, ensuring financial stability, or preparing for retirement, she expertly guides clients towards sound decisions and strategic investments that promise peace of mind and a brighter future.

A distinguished member of the Million Dollar Round Table (MDRT) for 17 years, Antonios has held key leadership roles within the organisation, including MDRT Country Chair for Lebanon (2019–2021) and Zone 12 Chair (2021–2023). Renowned for her intellectual prowess, innovative thinking, and leadership skills, Antonios inspires confidence in clients while fostering enduring relationships built on trust and excellence.

Introduction

In the financial advisory profession, especially within the life insurance sector, integrating scientific principles with emotional connections can significantly enhance the effectiveness of sales strategies. This chapter delves into the power of storytelling in shaping professional success, offering insights into how advisors can combine scientific and emotional elements for a successful sales approach.

The Scientific Foundation

Life insurance is a unique entity in the vast landscape of the insurance profession, intertwining science and emotion in a delicate dance. At its core, life insurance operates on actuarial principles and statistical analyses. Actuaries meticulously assess risks, mortality rates, and other factors to determine the appropriate premiums and coverage. The science behind life insurance is rooted in mathematical precision, ensuring a solid foundation for the financial protection it promises.

Advisors armed with this statistical knowledge become interpreters of risk for their clients. They dissect complex data into digestible insights, offering a clear picture of potential scenarios that might unfold. This scientific approach is the bedrock upon which clients build their trust, knowing that their decisions are informed by a rational understanding of probability and financial planning.

The Emotional Connection

Despite the scientific foundation, however, life insurance isn't merely a mathematical equation; it's a safeguard against the uncertainties of life. In the emotionally charged arena of family and personal well-being, advisors must empathise with clients and understand their fears, hopes, and aspirations. This emotional connection is the bridge that transforms life insurance from a cold, calculated transaction into a meaningful investment in the future.

Effective advisors recognise the importance of balancing facts and emotions during the sales cycle. They listen intently to clients' stories, asking probing questions to uncover the deeper motivations behind their insurance decisions. Whether it's ensuring a child's education, protecting a family home, or leaving a legacy, advisors empathise with the emotional core of their clients' needs.

Successful life insurance salesmanship thrives on the symbiosis between science and emotion. Advisors become educators, distilling complex concepts into relatable narratives that resonate with clients on a personal level. A well-crafted sales pitch weaves the logical risk mitigation framework with the emotional narrative of securing a family's future. Advisors guide clients through a journey that acknowledges both the head and the heart. Explaining the actuarial foundations with clarity and confidence lays the groundwork for trust, while tapping into the emotional aspects, thereby forging a connection beyond numbers on a policy document.

Emotion plays a crucial role in significant purchasing decisions. This is especially true for life insurance, which is an important decision. While emotion is typically a driving factor behind most decisions, few people recognise this. Most clients use logic to support their emotional decisions. The bottom line is that emotion is crucial to their choice. Simple stories will evoke that emotion effectively.

Storytelling is Story Selling

Storytelling is a powerful tool in the life insurance sales process, enabling advisors to convey information compellingly and relatably. By weaving stories into their presentations, advisors can engage clients, create emotional connections, and help individuals and families make informed decisions about their financial future. Here's how storytelling plays a crucial role in life insurance sales:

1. **Emotional connection:** Life insurance is a deeply personal and emotional decision. Stories tap into emotions, helping clients connect with the potential impact of life insurance on their own lives. Narratives about families facing unforeseen circumstances or stories of successful financial protection create empathy, making life insurance more tangible and relatable.

2. **Making complex concepts accessible:** Insurance policies can be complex and filled with technical details. Stories simplify these concepts, making them more accessible and understandable for clients. Using stories, advisors can break down intricate policy features into real-life scenarios, helping clients grasp the practical benefits without getting lost in the details.

3. **Building trust:** Trust is paramount in financial transactions, especially when they involve long-term commitments like life insurance. Stories serve as real-world evidence of the positive impact of life insurance. Sharing success stories and examples of how life insurance has provided security for other families builds trust by demonstrating its reliability and effectiveness.

4. **Addressing concerns and objections:** Clients often have concerns or objections about life insurance, such as cost, necessity, or understanding of the terms. Stories can directly address these concerns and dispel common misconceptions. Advisors can use stories to present scenarios that counter objections, providing reassurance and clarification. Real-life examples can address doubts and build confidence in the decision-making process.

5. **Motivating action:** Life insurance is often seen as a future-oriented decision. Stories inspire clients to take action by illustrating life insurance's long-term benefits and positive outcomes. Compelling narratives can motivate clients to consider the bigger picture, encouraging them to prioritise financial protection for their loved ones and make decisions that align with their long-term goals.

6. **Memorability and impact:** Stories are memorable. Clients are more likely to remember and resonate with a well-told story than a list of statistics or technical details. Advisors who incorporate storytelling into their presentations create a lasting impression. This increased memorability can influence clients' decision-making as they recall the emotional and practical aspects of the stories shared. A study found that only 5% of people remember statistics, compared to 63% who remember stories.

The Art of Selling: Create your Storyboards

Creating a compelling story during a life insurance sales cycle involves weaving a narrative that resonates with clients, making the concept of life insurance relatable and emotionally impactful. Here are the main pillars for crafting a successful story in the context of life insurance sales:

1. **Relevance to the client:**
   - *Know your audience:* Understand the client's background, aspirations, and concerns. Tailor the story to align with their specific life circumstances, making it relevant and relatable.
   - Example: If the client is a parent, share a story about how a family's financial security was protected after a parent's untimely death.
2. **Engagement:**
   - *Evoke emotions:* Engage the client emotionally by tapping into universal human experiences. Connect the story to themes of family, love, protection, and legacy.
   - Example: Share a story about how life insurance provided a safety net for a family during a challenging time, highlighting the emotional relief it brought.
3. **Realism and authenticity:**
   - *Use real-life examples:* Ground the story by using authentic examples. Clients are more likely to connect with stories that feel genuine and credible.
   - Example: Share challenges from actual client experiences, maintaining confidentiality but highlighting the positive outcomes achieved through life insurance.
4. **Overcoming challenges:**
   - *Highlight solutions:* Introduce challenges or obstacles that individuals or families face without life insurance, and then demonstrate how life insurance provided a solution.
   - Example: Illustrate a family struggling financially after a loss, emphasising how life insurance could have mitigated those difficulties.
5. **Educational value:**
   - *Incorporate teachable moments:* Use a story to educate clients about the importance and benefits of life insurance.

Break down complex concepts into understandable lessons.

- o Example: Explain how a particular plan could address specific financial needs, using the story as a practical illustration.

6. **Positive outcomes:**
   - o *Focus on success:* Emphasise the positive outcomes and benefits of life insurance.
   - o Example: Conclude the story by highlighting how the family in the narrative was able to maintain their lifestyle and achieve long-term goals because of life insurance.

7. **Client as the protagonist:**
   - o *Make the client the hero:* Position the client as the central figure in the story, emphasising their role in securing their loved ones' well-being.
   - o Example: Craft a narrative where the client is the proactive decision-maker, taking steps to protect their family's future.

8. **Clarity and simplicity:**
   - o *Avoid technical words:* Keep the story simple, avoiding complex industry terms that may confuse or overwhelm the client.
   - o Example: Use plain language to describe policy features and benefits, ensuring the client easily understands the key takeaways.

9. **Call to action:**
   - o *Inspire action:* Conclude the story with a clear call to action, encouraging the client to consider how they can secure their family's future through life insurance.
   - o Example: Prompt the client to discuss their specific needs and explore suitable life insurance options based on the insights gained from the story.

Crafting a successful story involves a delicate balance of emotional engagement, educational content, and a focus on positive outcomes. By incorporating these pillars into your storytelling during the sales cycle, you can create a narrative that resonates with clients and motivates them to make informed decisions about their financial security.

Crafting a Compelling Story

Here's a suggested structure for crafting a compelling story:

1. **Set the stage:**
   - Capture the client's attention and establish the story's context.
   - Include an intriguing opening that sparks interest.
   - Briefly introduce the characters and setting.
   - Establish the theme or challenge that the story will address.
2. **Introduce the challenge:**
   - Present the character's problem or challenge, emphasising its importance.
   - Clearly define the problem or challenge.
   - Evoke empathy by connecting the challenge to everyday human experiences.
   - Make the client aware of the potential risks and consequences.
3. **Explore the consequences:**
   - Develop the story by delving into the consequences of not addressing the challenge.
   - Unfold the story, revealing the escalating challenges.
   - Describe the emotional toll on the characters.
   - Introduce financial hardships and uncertainties.

4. **Set the stage:**
   - Capture the client's attention and establish the story's context.
   - Include an intriguing opening that sparks interest.
   - Briefly introduce the characters and setting.
   - Establish the theme or challenge that the story will address.

5. **Introduce the challenge:**
   - Present the character's problem or challenge, emphasising its importance.
   - Clearly define the problem or challenge.
   - Evoke empathy by connecting the challenge to everyday human experiences.
   - Make the client aware of the potential risks and consequences.

6. **Explore the consequences:**
   - Develop the story by delving into the consequences of not addressing the challenge.
   - Unfold the story, revealing the escalating challenges.
   - Describe the emotional toll on the characters.
   - Introduce financial hardships and uncertainties.

7. **Turning point:**
   - Introduce life insurance as the solution to the challenges presented in the story.
   - Clearly explain how life insurance can address specific challenges.
   - Highlight the benefits of life insurance in mitigating risks.
   - Emphasise the transformative role life insurance can play.

8. **Explain key concepts:**
   - Provide essential information about life insurance in straightforward and understandable terms.
   - Break down complex concepts into simple, relatable terms.

o Use the story's characters to illustrate the practical application of different life insurance features.

9. **Positive outcomes:**
   o Showcase the positive outcomes and benefits of life insurance.
   o Describe how life insurance positively impacted the characters' lives.
   o Illustrate financial security, peace of mind, and the ability to pursue long-term goals.
   o Emphasise the emotional relief experienced by the characters.

10. **Reflection and consideration:**
   o Allow the client to reflect on the story and consider its relevance to their life.
   o Provide a moment for the client to absorb the story's impact.
   o Encourage reflection on their financial goals and family's well-being.
   o Set the stage for the client to consider life insurance actively.

11. **Resolution:**
   o Inspire the client to consider life insurance options.
   o Clearly state the call to action, such as scheduling a follow-up meeting or discussing specific policies.
   o Reinforce the client's role as the proactive decision-maker.
   o Express confidence that life insurance can be a positive and transformative choice for their family's future.

12. **Reiterate the importance:**
   o Reinforce the story's importance and relevance to the client's life.
   o Summarise the key takeaways from the story.
   o Express gratitude for the client's time and engagement.

- Leave a lasting impression, emphasising the significance of life insurance in securing their family's future.

When to Tell your Story

The timing of storytelling during the sales cycle is crucial for maximum impact. The goal is to engage and educate the client, making the information about life insurance relatable and memorable. Here are key points during the sales cycle when storytelling can be effectively incorporated:

1. **Introduction and icebreaking:**
   - *Purpose:* Capture the client's attention and establish rapport.
   - *When:* At the beginning of the meeting or presentation.
   - *How:* Start with a compelling and relevant story to create an immediate connection. This helps set a positive tone for the conversation.
2. **Needs analysis:**
   - *Purpose:* Understand the client's concerns, goals, and financial situation.
   - *When:* After initial introductions and before diving into policy details.
   - *How:* Use stories to illustrate scenarios that align with the client's potential needs, allowing them to see the practical application of life insurance in addressing their concerns.
3. **Educational interlude:**
   - *Purpose:* Provide information about life insurance concepts and policies.
   - *When:* After the initial needs analysis.
   - *How:* Incorporate stories to explain key concepts, making

the information more accessible and relatable. Use real-life examples to illustrate policy features.

4. **Addressing concerns and objections:**
   - *Purpose:* Overcome potential objections or misconceptions.
   - *When:* As objections arise during the discussion.
   - *How:* Share stories that directly address common concerns. Use examples of how life insurance has addressed similar objections in real-life situations.

5. **Building emotional connection:**
   - *Purpose:* Forge a deeper emotional connection with the client.
   - *When:* Throughout the presentation, especially when discussing the potential consequences of not having life insurance.
   - *How:* Share emotionally resonant stories that highlight the impact of life insurance on families, emphasising the emotional relief and security it provides.

6. **Illustrating policy options:**
   - *Purpose:* Explain different policy options and their benefits.
   - *When:* When introducing specific policy details.
   - *How:* Use stories to illustrate how different policy options have worked for others, making it easier for the client to visualise the practical application of each option.

7. **Culmination and decision-making:**
   - *Purpose:* Encourage the client to make informed decisions.
   - *When:* Towards the end of the presentation.
   - *How:* Share success stories reinforcing positive outcomes from life insurance decisions. This helps motivate the client to see life insurance as a valuable and transformative choice.

8. **Closing and next steps:**
    - *Purpose:* Wrap up the meeting and guide the client towards the next steps.
    - *When:* At the end of the presentation.
    - *How:* Conclude with a story summarising key points and reinforcing the importance of action. Clearly state the next steps, such as scheduling a follow-up meeting or initiating the application process.

By strategically incorporating storytelling at these key points during the sales cycle, you can enhance engagement, address concerns, and guide clients towards making informed decisions about their life insurance needs.

Conclusion

Storytelling is a powerful tool that can transform the sales process in the life insurance profession. By combining scientific principles with emotional narratives, advisors can build trust, simplify complex concepts, address concerns, and motivate clients to act. Crafting compelling stories and strategically incorporating them throughout the sales cycle can lead to deeper client connections, informed decision-making, and professional success.

Part Four
Client Relations and Trust Building

Chapter 10
Purpose Decides the Choice
Jayang Nagrecha

Jayang Nagrecha, fondly known as Jango, is a celebrated financial planner recognised for his dedication to the profession and his ability to connect with people from all walks of life. Born in India, Jango's journey reflects his relentless pursuit of excellence and personal growth.

Armed with a Bachelor of Commerce (B.Com.) and diplomas in International Trade Management (DITM) and Financial Services and Investment Management (DFSIM), Jango has built a solid foundation for his career. He is a 13-time Million Dollar Round Table (MDRT) qualifier and has served on various MDRT committees, contributing significantly to the global financial planning community. As a sought-after speaker, he has delivered impactful sessions at prestigious events like the Connexion Zone in Boston and the Focus Session in Singapore.

Outside of his professional achievements, Jango is an adventurer and a passionate mountaineer who has scaled Himalayan peaks and reached the base of Mount Everest. A solo traveller and marathon runner, he embodies resilience and determination in all aspects of life. Guided by his mantra, "Where there is a will, there is a way, and where there is no way, Jango makes his way," he continues to inspire others with his story of innovation and perseverance.

Introduction

This picture shows an airplane flying from Dubai to London, which unexpectedly encountered some very bad weather. Have you ever seen a pilot divert a plane to Italy, Spain, or France from a similar flight path?

Usually, the answer is no, unless there is a severe emergency. Instead, the pilot will either ascend to a much higher altitude or descend to a lower altitude to avoid the storm, but in the end, they will reach their prescribed destination.

Similarly, in our lives, do situations like this prevail or not? Our lives often face turbulence or rainy days, which come and go. What do we generally do in such instances?

For the majority of us, we usually land in a different place to what we had planned. This happens mainly because our lives are not purpose driven, which is exactly what they should be.

Your purpose should always determine your choices.

In the last 24 years that I've spent in the financial services profession, the following questions have been very common:

- "Where should I invest my money now to grow and multiply it in the best way? Is this the right time?"
- "The present trend is that most people I meet are investing in mutual funds, and I feel that I'm missing this wagon. Should I do that now?"
- "Are equities at their peak now? There may be a decline in the future, so should I wait or invest now?"
- "A huge amount of taxes are saved as per the new income tax law in the form of principal payments and rebates given for interest payments. Should I apply for a housing loan, buy a house, and let it out for rent? From the rent, I can pay the EMIs (equated monthly instalments), and the appreciation of the property will be very high. Do you think I should do that?"
- "Someone told me that futures, derivatives, and option trading give good returns. Even in a falling market, they perform well. Should I invest a little money in that?
- "Should I put money into cryptocurrency or not?"
- "Can you suggest a good investment? I'm ready to invest a lump sum of ₹25 lakh (₹2.5 million) within the next week."

What is more surprising is that, many times, even people engaged in financial markets ask me these questions—bankers, advisors of mutual funds, small savings scheme representatives, and personnel from regulatory offices.

Purpose Over Asset Selection

These questions cannot be answered meaningfully without under-standing the purpose of the investment. Before deciding on an asset, the following questions should be asked:

1. When will I require this money back?
2. How much will I require then?
3. For what purpose will I require that money?
4. How long do I want to invest this money (tenure)?

Cash 2 Cash Cycle

Take a look at this picture, which is called the Cash 2 Cash Cycle:

A person works hard and earns money. From that money, they buy assets (like mutual funds, property, gold, insur-ance policies, etc.). Over time, they convert these assets into cash to fulfil their various needs.

One thing becomes clear from this picture: **"Cash is king; assets are intermediaries."**

There are only two uses for assets:

1. To produce cash (investment assets).
2. To be used for comfort, image, or happiness (personal assets).

Personal Assets vs Investment Assets

Personal assets—like a residential house, jewellery, cars, and gadgets—are bought for comfort, happiness, or to create a good image in society.

Investment assets are bought with the sole intention of converting them into cash at a later time.

If that is the case, the above questions (*When will I require this back? How much will I require then? For what purpose will I require that money?*) must be answered before selecting assets that will serve the purpose.

To do so, we need to draw a **map of our life** and mark the junctions where we will require money.

The Importance of a Life Map

What does any map contain? Paths, terrains, and legends.

Why do we need a map for our future? Because we have never been there before.

In general, a person with a map can navigate better than one without it. Look at this example:

Jayang Nagrecha

Say that I am travelling on a metro train in Dubai, boarding at Centre-point Station, with my destination being Jabeel Ali. If I have this map in my hand, I can peacefully listen to music or read a book during my journey. Without the map, I would find myself enquiring with my neighbours before and after every station. Some might guide me correctly, but others may not. Even that 45-minute journey would be full of tension without a map.

If just 45 minutes of travel without a map can be so stressful, how would it feel to live your entire life without a map?

The Roads of Life

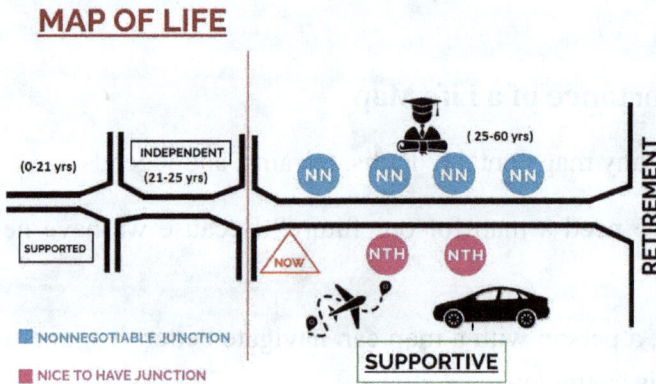

MAP OF LIFE

Our life map begins with three distinct roads:

1. **Supported road (Age 0 to 21):**

This is the stage where we are financially dependent on our parents or guardians. Whatever we need or ask for is provided by them.

2. **Independent road (Age 21 to 25):**

This short road begins with our first job, business, or any other means of earning an income. It's a time of independence, happiness, and newfound responsibilities.

3. **Supportive road (Age 25 to 60):**

This is the longest road, where we earn an income and take on responsibilities such as caring for our spouse, planning for our children's education, providing for our retirement, and supporting aging parents.

Navigating the Supportive Road

On the supportive road, we need to:

1. **Mark junctions:**

Identify times when we will require lump-sum money. For example:

- Age 30: Childbirth
- Age 35: Buying a car
- Age 38: Buying an apartment
- Age 40: A tour to Europe
- Age 48: Children's higher education
- Age 50: Resigning from a job to start a business

2. **Plan contributions:**

Determine how much money can be saved each year in a disciplined way towards paying for these junctions, and how much we currently have to start with.

3. **Estimate requirements:**

Calculate how much money will be required in order to afford each junction.

4. **Categorise junctions:**

Divide them into:

- **Non-negotiable goals:**

Goals that cannot be compromised, like funding children's education or retirement. For example, you cannot delay a child's education just because the stock market is down.

- **Nice-to-have goals:**

Goals that are negotiable and can be postponed, such as buying a new car or going on a foreign tour.

5. **Choose suitable assets:**

Select assets that will help achieve the identified junctions. If funds are insufficient, prioritise non-negotiable goals and reduce the focus on nice-to-have goals.

Purpose-driven Decisions

Without purpose, asset accumulation does not bring happiness. Consider this example:

A person buys land for ₹25 lakhs (₹2.5 million) and sells it ten years later for ₹1 crore (₹10 million). While they are happy with the profit, they feel disappointed when the buyer sells the same land three months later for ₹1.1 crore (₹11 million). Why does this happen?

The land was bought without a specific purpose, so emotions take over. However, if the land had been purchased to fund a child's higher education, achieving that purpose would overshadow any regrets about missed profits.

This emotional turbulence occurs in reverse as well. For example, if the second buyer sells the land for ₹90 lakhs (₹9 million) due to an emergency, the first seller feels lucky for selling at the right time.

Such randomness in selecting assets blinds logic, often leading to regret.

Benefits of Purpose-driven Investments

1. Risk management:

Purpose helps determine the risk level tolerable for a goal. Non-negotiable goals require lower-risk products, while nice-to-have goals can handle higher risk.

2. Timespan clarity:

Purpose sets the holding period for assets, enabling better choices and preventing panic during volatile times.

Jayang Nagrecha

3. Progress satisfaction:

Purpose provides happiness when regular investments align with financial plans, creating a sense of achievement.

Risk Tolerance and Safety

When the purpose of investing is known, the risk tolerance level for that goal becomes clear.

What is risk?

Risk is the probability of loss or the negative variation between expected and actual outcomes. The opposite of safety, risk needs to be carefully managed to ensure that investments align with goals.

Conclusion

Purpose should always drive decisions and investments. When investments are purpose-driven, they lead to desired goals, minimise emotional upheaval, and create lasting satisfaction. By understanding the purpose behind every financial decision, you not only achieve your objectives but also gain peace of mind along the way.

My special thanks to my guru, respected **Shri R Gopinath**, who has always mentored me and showered me with his blessings.

Chapter 11
The Art of Data Gathering
Ravi Rajpal

Ravi Rajpal is a seasoned financial coach with over 23 years of experience in wealth management, consistently guiding individuals and families towards financial security. A 23-time Million Dollar Round Table (MDRT) qualifier, Ravi's achievements include seven Court of the Table (COT) honours, placing him among the top 1% of financial advisors globally.

Ravi's approach focuses on educating and empowering clients, helping them to understand how their savings contribute to long-term security. Serving 600 families with a 100% persistency ratio, he and his team deliver lifelong service rooted in trust and transparency. His life's mission is to create abundance for all while inspiring others to think and act beyond the ordinary.

Ravi Rajpal

As MDRT Zone Chair, Ravi has trained financial advisors in India and Southeast Asia for over a decade. He has addressed more than 9,000 advisors worldwide and contributes to the MDRT Academy, creating training content to elevate the profession. A sought-after speaker, Ravi has delivered impactful presentations globally.

Beyond his profession, Ravi is passionate about fitness and nutrition. A black belt martial artist and state swimmer, he finds inspiration from his family. Through his leadership and dedication, Ravi leaves a lasting legacy of financial empowerment and growth.

Introduction

Data gathering in financial planning is not just a technical task of collecting information; it is the first step towards building a meaningful advisor-client relationship. It involves delving into the intimate details of a client's financial life, uncovering their dreams, challenges, and priorities. Finances are often tied to some of the most personal and emotional aspects of life, including family, career, health, and future aspirations. As such, data gathering requires sensitivity, empathy, and professionalism.

For advisors, mastering the art of data gathering is essential. The process forms the foundation for creating personalised financial plans, identifying opportunities, and building trust with clients. It is not simply about assembling numbers—it is about understanding the human story behind the data. This chapter explores the techniques, benefits, and nuances of effective data gathering, offering practical advice for transforming raw information into actionable insights that serve both the client and the advisor.

The Emotional Connection

Imagine asking someone to reveal their deepest financial hopes, fears, and uncertainties. For many clients, discussing finances is a deeply personal and vulnerable experience. Financial matters are rarely just about money—they are tied to emotions, relationships, and life goals. Establishing an emotional connection with clients is therefore critical for fostering trust and openness.

Understanding the Client's Perspective

Clients approach financial discussions with different emotional states. Some may feel confident and eager to share their goals, while others may be hesitant or even ashamed of their financial situations. Advisors must meet clients where they are emotionally, creating a non-judgmental environment that encourages openness. For example:

- A client burdened by debt may feel embarrassed to discuss their struggles. An empathetic approach, focusing on solutions rather than past mistakes, can help them feel supported.
- Another client may feel anxious about securing their family's future. Validating their concerns and reassuring them that these challenges are common can build rapport.

Recognising the emotional context behind financial decisions helps advisors tailor their approach and connect with clients on a deeper level.

Preparation and Mindset

Before meeting with a client, advisors should reflect on their mindset. Viewing the client as a unique individual with valuable goals and experiences ensures that the advisor approaches the conversation with curiosity and respect. This preparation helps the advisor focus on understanding the client's perspective rather than rushing to provide solutions.

Additionally, advisors must commit to a service-oriented mindset. By prioritising the client's success and well-being, they establish themselves as trusted partners in the client's financial journey.

Creating a Safe Space

Building trust begins with creating an environment where clients feel safe sharing personal information. Advisors should emphasise confidentiality and explain how the data will be used to benefit the client. For example:

"Our discussion today will help me understand your financial picture so that I can create a plan tailored to your goals. Everything you share will remain private."

This reassurance fosters a sense of security and encourages clients to engage openly.

Long-Term Benefits of Emotional Connection

The emotional connection built during initial data gathering often extends throughout the advisor-client relationship. Clients who feel understood are more likely to maintain long-term engagement, trust the advisor's recommendations, and seek advice for future milestones. This deep connection ensures a partnership built on mutual respect and shared goals.

Advantages of Data Gathering

Data gathering is not merely an administrative task—it is the corner-stone of effective financial planning. By collecting and analysing comprehensive client information, advisors unlock numerous benefits that enhance the quality of their services and the strength of their rela-tionships.

1. Understanding the Client

Understanding a client's financial picture requires looking beyond numbers to uncover the motivations, fears, and aspirations driving their decisions. For example:

- A client saving aggressively for retirement may prioritise financial independence and a secure future.
- Another client may focus on preserving wealth to provide for their children and future generations.

How this Translates into Practice

- Gather insights into the client's financial goals to create a roadmap that balances short-term needs with long-term ambitions.
- Uncover the emotional reasons behind financial behaviours, such as cautious spending habits or an aversion to risk, to provide empathetic and relevant advice.
- Use understanding to strengthen the advisor-client relationship, ensuring the client feels heard and valued.

Ravi Rajpal

2. Tailored Solutions

Personalised solutions resonate more deeply with clients than generic advice. Data gathering allows advisors to design customised strategies that reflect the client's circumstances, life stage, and aspirations. For instance:

- A young professional might prioritise growth-focused investments and saving for a home.
- A retiree may focus on generating passive income and preserving capital.

Examples of Tailored Solutions

- Advisors might recommend tax-efficient investments for a high-income client seeking to minimise liabilities while maximising returns.
- A family-focused client might benefit from education savings plans or insurance policies to protect their loved ones in the event of unforeseen circumstances.
- A business person may want estate and legacy planning.
- We should ask the client how they want their money to work for them.
- Support the client to prioritise their financial goals and cash flow.

3. Trust Building

Clients are more likely to trust advisors who take the time to listen, understand, and personalise their advice. By gathering and analysing detailed client information, advisors show their dedication to the client's success. This trust creates a foundation for long-term relationships, encouraging clients to share more candidly and seek ongoing guidance. We have to be very vocal in letting the client know that whatever they share will be kept completely confidential.

Building Trust Through Transparency

Advisors can strengthen trust by clearly explaining how they will use the collected data to create tailored plans. Providing regular updates and follow-ups on financial strategies further reinforces the client's confidence in the advisor's expertise and commitment.

4. Opportunity Identification

Comprehensive data collection often reveals gaps in the client's financial strategy or opportunities for additional services. For example:

- A client without adequate insurance may benefit from a discussion about protecting their family's future.
- A business owner may require advice on succession planning to ensure the continuity of their operations.
- Data collection also gets us to know the nature and risk appetite of the prospect.
- We even get to know about the client's relationship with money and their expectations.
- It's important to let the client know that it's their responsibility to share data relating to lifestyle changes that can occur in the future, such as:
  - being blessed with a child
  - deciding to change jobs
  - losing a job or taking a pay cut or increment in salary
  - receiving a bonus or windfall
  - experiencing profit or loss in their business
  - gaining a new partner in life

- having their parents retire, or retiring themselves
- plans to purchase a house, car, weekend home, or any asset that may impact their cash flow

Expanding the Client's Horizon

Many clients are unaware of the range of financial tools and strategies available to them. Data gathering helps advisors introduce clients to options they may not have considered, such as estate planning, investment diversification, or retirement income strategies. Clients are good at making and conserving money. We need to partner with them to help them manage and multiply their savings.

Proper asset allocation will encourage to client to increase their nett worth.

5. Risk Profile Awareness

Understanding a client's risk tolerance is critical for designing appropriate investment strategies. By exploring the client's comfort level with risk, advisors can create portfolios that balance growth and stability. For example:

- A client with a low risk tolerance may prefer conservative investments like bonds and fixed-income securities.
- A client with a high risk tolerance may explore equities, real estate, or emerging markets.
- Clients should know we are great with managing risk and not returns.

Strategies for Identifying Risk Tolerance

- Use hypothetical scenarios to gauge how a client might respond to market fluctuations.
- Discuss past financial experiences to understand how they influence the client's current approach to risk.
- Provide clear explanations of risk levels associated with different investment options to empower informed decision-making.

Beginning the Conversation

Starting a financial conversation can feel daunting for clients, particularly if they fear judgement or feel unprepared. Advisors must approach these discussions with empathy, creating an environment where clients feel comfortable sharing their concerns and goals.

Setting the Stage

Begin by explaining the purpose of the conversation and reassuring the client about confidentiality. For example:

"Let's discuss your financial goals and how I can help you achieve them. Everything we talk about will remain private and will only be used to create a plan tailored to your needs," or, "I will ask you questions relating to your financial situation and what you want your future to look like in terms of money."

Such statements set a positive and non-threatening tone, encouraging clients to engage openly.

Ask Foundational Questions

Start with straightforward questions to establish context and gather basic information:

- What is your age?
- Are you married, and do you have children?
- Do you have anyone else financially dependent on you?

These questions provide a foundation for deeper discussions about the client's responsibilities and aspirations.

Exploring Goals

Introduce common financial goals to help clients identify their own objectives. Examples include:

- Buying a home
- Saving for children's education
- Planning for retirement

Encourage clients to elaborate by asking:

- What other financial dreams do you have?
- How would you prioritise these goals?

These discussions help clients articulate their objectives, providing valuable insights for the advisor.

Data Collection

Once the conversation is underway, advisors can gather more detailed information. Each question should be expanded upon to ensure thorough understanding and insight.

Who Relies on you Financially?

Dependents shape financial priorities. This could include children, elderly parents, or even extended family. Clarify these relationships by asking:

- Are your children in school or university?
- Do you assist ageing parents with medical or living expenses?
- Are there other commitments, such as supporting a sibling or funding a family business?

What Influenced your Current Investment Choices?

Understanding past decisions provides insight into the client's financial personality. Ask:

- Were these investments recommended by someone you trust?
- Do they align with your current goals, or have your priorities shifted?

What are your Hobbies and Passions?

Personal interests often shape financial goals. For example:

- A client who loves travel may need a dedicated fund for trips.
- A collector may allocate resources to expanding their collection.

Utilising the Data

The data collected during these discussions is more than just information—it's a living resource that evolves as the client's circumstances change. Advisors should use this data to craft tailored solutions, strengthen relationships, and proactively adjust plans to keep them relevant.

Tailored Solutions

Create financial plans that align with the client's unique goals, values, and priorities. For example:

> *"Based on your goal of retiring early, we'll focus on maximising savings and investing in growth opportunities over the next decade."*

Conclusion

Data gathering is not merely a task but a critical art in financial advising. By understanding clients' unique circumstances, building trust, identifying opportunities, and creating personalised strategies, advisors can transform this process into a powerful tool for fostering long-term relationships and delivering meaningful results.

When approached with empathy and professionalism, data gathering becomes the foundation of financial success for both the client and the advisor. Through consistent refinement and active engagement, advisors can ensure that their clients' financial plans remain dynamic and effective for years to come.

Chapter 12
Build and Grow – Relationships Lead to Business

Dr Sijo C. Mathews HC

Dr Sijo C. Mathews HC is a proud navy veteran turned accomplished financial advisor who has been empowering individuals and families to achieve financial freedom since 2010. With a doctorate in financial planning and wealth management, 14 years of industry expertise, and a stellar track record that includes MDRT qualifications (13 years) and prestigious Top of the Table honours, he's a trailblazer in income protection and wealth preservation.

A former MCC Country Chair for the UAE (2021–2024) and Zurich's Insurance Educator of the Year, Sijo combines discipline and vision to deliver exceptional results, managing a $94 million portfolio spanning six continents. When he's not guiding clients or creating financial awareness on social media, you'll find him exploring the world, remixing tracks as a closet DJ, or volunteering with animal rescue initiatives alongside his wife, Vineetha.

Known as the "Insurance Godfather," Sijo crafts and offers insurance and investment solutions no one can refuse. The kind that secures promises, protects incomes, and prepares for life's uncertainties.

Introduction

Insurance is one profession that thrives on relationships. The connections we build with clients strengthen over time and contribute significantly to business growth. Life insurance is a field where relationships play a pivotal role. As insurance advisors, our role extends beyond selling policies; it involves maintaining relationships through services like premium collections and investment realignments. The belief that relationships drive business, and vice versa, has been a cornerstone of my successful career.

The Power of Genuine Relationships

I've witnessed substantial business coming from unexpected sources simply because of the genuine relationships formed with no ulterior motives. It's a two-way street—relationships bring in more business, and business, in turn, strengthens relationships.

Some advisors express reluctance to engage in business with friends and family, a sentiment I find perplexing. Why not leverage the advantage of selling insurance to those who trust us, understand our lives, and can benefit from personalised advice? This hesitancy may stem from a lack of confidence in the service provided. If an advisor believes in the product, there should be no hesitation in offering it to friends and family.

Long-standing professional advisors often find that their inner circle comprises friends and family. While this is a common sentiment, it underscores the importance of building and maintaining relationships within our personal and professional networks. My family and inner circle have played a significant role in my growth, and I am eternally grateful to them.

My Journey in the UAE

My insurance journey in the UAE started in 2010. Being recruited to an insurance brokerage in Dubai was my stepping stone. After a miserable and failed attempt in business back home in India, I used the pretext of life insurance sales as an entry to the UAE, and then turned it into a successful profession and career. After a few months in Dubai, I vividly remember my mother-in-law asking my wife if I had found a decent career yet. Today, she's proud of me and the service I provide.

I started with cold calls and meetings, as we all do. With time and hard work, my business slowly grew. It wasn't easy but definitely was rewarding. I could, and am able to, do so much that I only dreamt of. When my client base expanded, so did the challenges of selling and servicing simultaneously. I realised the need for assistance but couldn't afford a full-time assistant.

Innovation Through Relationships

I really needed help, as I was unable to make cold calls, conduct meetings, and do my follow-ups at the same time. Of course, my company was providing administrative support, but I felt I needed more; my clients deserved more. I wanted to be out meeting people instead of sitting in the office.

I could not afford to hire an assistant, which, let me tell you, is an incredible added value to your image in the minds of both clients and prospects. There is nothing more efficient and professional than having an assistant make your calls and fill up your schedule. This fact was very clear in my mind; but another fact was equally loud and clear—I could not afford a full-time assistant.

A Creative Solution

Here is when being innovative and looking towards your relationships can save your career. I have my better half at home, who had worked in an international call centre and later as an HR administrator for 12 years. She had to take a career break to care for my father after my mum passed away in 2010, the same year we landed in the UAE. Over the years, she had already acquired a fair knowledge of my business by listening to my calls. With her call centre background, she wouldn't need much training, and above all, I could rely on her 100%.

Now, I still couldn't afford an assistant, but a part-time cook and cleaner was not difficult. My wife was more than happy to be free of the housework, and I hit two birds with one stone: have a very happy wife and an assistant too! I trained her, assigned her the cold calls, fixed my appointments, and followed up with my clients. She was even happier because now she knows exactly where I am and who I am meeting at every moment of my day. My personal GPS tracker.

Believe these words: when she calls and introduces herself as the insurance coordinator for Dr Sijo Mathews, my image gets upgraded in the minds of my clients, and somehow, the appointment cancellation rate drops significantly when someone else is booking it for you.

As with everything else in life, there is a catch here too. Over the years, she has become so good that she started getting job offers from many clients and prospects, which I knew she was seriously considering. However, knowing that I am now able to afford a younger personal assistant made her reject all those offers. Besides, her job with me includes travelling the world for free, so she is still on board. That's using your existing relationships to enhance business.

Lifelong Relationships

Sometimes lifelong relationships are formed out of the blue. One incident exemplifies the importance of using the opportunity for establishing strong relationships. How far are we willing to go to establish ourselves as trusted and indispensable partners in our clients' minds? For me, it meant going above and beyond what was expected.

Going the Extra Mile

There was one notable incident—a first meeting with a big prospect. I sensed that he was tense and worried about something, so I turned the conversation from the main purpose, financial planning, to make it about him. As we insurance advisors happen to be good listeners, he felt he could share too, so he opened up and told me that he was concerned about a document relating to a major real estate deal that needed to be delivered to Mumbai the next day. It was a weekend night, and none of the courier companies were able to accept the consignment with guaranteed delivery before lunch the next day.

What would you do if you were in my shoes? Without hesitation, I offered to have it delivered for him. With a surprising look, he asked, *"Would you really do that for me?"* I responded, *"You have no idea what I can do for you, sir."* He had nothing to lose and knew that being up and around in the market all the time, I might have contacts that could probably make it happen.

Well, that wasn't exactly how it happened, though. I flew to Mumbai the same night, delivered the document, and returned home, incurring a cost of AED 1,870 ($500), which I did not charge it to the client, though he would have been more than happy to pay twice the amount. Had I taken the money, I would have just been a glorified courier.

The value of the relationship that I established with him over the next 10 years was priceless. I earned significant income from the relationship and several referrals, but the best part was the way he always introduced me to others:

> *"This is that chap that flew to Mumbai as my courier, and you have no idea what he can do for you."*

Acknowledging that similar attempts have been made by others, I won't claim sole ownership of this idea. I vaguely remember reading about a similar audacious service by a salesman somewhere, but apparently, my client hadn't read that book.

Building Trust with Business Clients

Another lesson on relationships bringing in business unfolded in 2012 with a businessman client. Over a period of time, we had built a good relationship, and my office was servicing his company for most of their insurance business. Since I was visiting his office often, I was a familiar face for his staff, and was known as the insurance guy. They used to ask questions about insurance and investments back home, which I happily answered. There was a coffee shop in the same building, and I would often have tea and snacks with staff members discussing family and even insurance-related matters. A few of them had even made small-term plans with me; one was Mr M, the family and company driver.

One day, Mr M was driving his boss's friend, Mr K, who had just arrived in Dubai. On the way to the hotel, the friend was on the phone talking to someone about some insurance matter and seemed upset. Mr M, having been with the company for over 10 years, was well known to the boss's friend too. At some point, Mr M asked if he was having trouble with insurance and if he needed assistance. He said that he knew this gentleman, Mr Mathews, who does insurance; maybe he can assist you. Well, Mr K asked if he understood what the requirement was, for this he got the reply:

> *"I am not sure, but if it's insurance and Mr Mathews can't do it for you, he will definitely guide you to the right person."*

Long story short, my contact details were shared, and I ended up closing the first, and one of the highest, mortgage insurance policies in my career. Since then, I have done much more business with Mr K, all thanks to the trust and confidence of one person who hardly knew anything about what I did. Another important point to note here is that this was a big company, and they were dealing with several other insurance advisors for different services, and Mr M knew everyone. Later, when I asked him why he recommended me and not any of the others, all he said was, *"Sir, you are always nice to us."*

Relationships with Colleagues and Competitors

Another essential aspect of business relationships is the rapport with colleagues and even competitors. Many might view competitors strictly as adversaries, but in the insurance profession, this isn't always the case. Building respectful and cordial relationships with competitors can sometimes lead to mutually beneficial situations.

For instance, there have been occasions where I received referrals from competitors who were unable to meet a particular client's needs due to constraints on their side. Similarly, I've referred clients to competitors when I believed they could provide a better service for that client's specific needs. This reciprocity builds a network of trust and respect within the profession, ultimately benefiting everyone involved.

Within our own organisations, fostering positive relationships with colleagues is equally important. Collaboration and knowledge sharing can significantly enhance our effectiveness as advisors. I've found that working closely with colleagues, sharing insights, and providing mutual support not only improves our individual performance but also creates a more cohesive and successful team.

The Role of Professional Development

Continuous professional development is another critical aspect of main-taining and growing business relationships. Staying updated on the latest trends, products, and regulations in the insurance profession is essential. By doing so, we can provide our clients with the best possible advice and solutions, reinforcing their trust in our expertise.

Attending industry conferences, participating in workshops, and pursuing advanced certifications are all valuable ways to enhance our knowledge and skills. These activities also provide opportunities to network with other professionals, share experiences, and learn from each other. The more knowledgeable and competent we are, the more confident our clients will be in our abilities, further strengthening our relationships with them.

Leveraging Technology to Enhance Relationships

In today's digital age, leveraging technology is indispensable for enhancing business relationships. Customer relationship management (CRM) systems, for example, allow us to keep detailed records of client interactions, preferences, and needs. This information enables us to personalise our services and communications, making our clients feel valued and understood.

Social media platforms are also powerful tools for building and maintaining relationships. By engaging with clients and prospects on social media, we can stay connected, share relevant content, and respond promptly to their inquiries and concerns. Regularly posting updates about our services, industry news, and success stories helps keep our clients informed and engaged.

There was a social media session I attended where the speaker said one important thing:

> *"If and when you post on social media—don't let it be an attempt to sell—share information and free awareness. Connect and encourage people to engage."*

How many people post on social media in their local language? I do, and let me tell you, the engagement I've received through my Malayalam videos has been phenomenal. We often assume that our ideal prospects aren't spending time on Instagram looking for life insurance and investment tips. You might be right, but here's the thing: behind every individual is a family—wives, husbands, children.

You wouldn't believe how many women have seen my posts and approached me, starting with casual conversations that evolved into full family meetings to discuss financial planning. It's amazing how these connections grow and transform lives.

The first and best return on investment (ROI) from my renewed social media activity came from a cousin who boldly admitted she didn't realise I was involved in education planning. She's now one of my clients.

Our posts aren't just seen—they're followed, liked, and commented on. A simple question in a direct message can turn into a full meeting. And there is a big advantage here—when you're connected with a prospective client on social media—be it Instagram, Facebook, or LinkedIn—you gain valuable insights about them: their family, travel plans, hobbies, and more.

That's our advantage. Yes, relationships for insurance can also be built through social media. Some might call it stalking, but we professionals call it fact-finding.

When building your personal brand, strive to create something unique that sets you apart. A strong, recognisable brand not only makes you memorable but also helps establish trust and credibility in your industry. I've positioned myself as the **Insurance Godfather**, a brand identity that resonates with my audience and reinforces my expertise. This distinct branding has significantly enhanced my visibility and made it easier for people to connect with me and my services. Your personal brand should reflect your values, expertise, and personality—something that people instantly associate with you.

There's one crucial thing I need to emphasise—your posts must include you, including your face. At the very least, provide an introduction about what the content is going to be. People need to know your face.

So, when you finally meet that prospect, they're already warmed up. You save time on introductions and dive right into meaningful conversations. You finish the meeting on a positive note, and guess what? Seven out of ten times, they'll check you out again if they haven't already. It's happened to me, and it can happen to you. That's why having a strong LinkedIn profile is essential.

Digital Innovation in Client Interaction

At a random meeting, we present our business cards. How many of you get the feeling that a client won't look at the card once you leave? I have had that many times. Now, who would like to end a client meeting with their contact info and even entire bio on the client's phone before they leave? Would you agree if I said that the odds of being remembered, referred, or connected are way higher if your number is stored on the client's phone and not left in their office drawer?

The answer is a digital card with a QR code and NFC. It's also classy.

Never give a client your card anymore. Help them scan or tap and connect; even better, do it for them and add an extension like "insurance guy" to your name. Trust me, it will make it a lot easier for you to be found with "insurance" than looking for your name. There it is, easily accessible until the relationship is built and you are known by your name and not just the service.

Additionally, virtual meeting tools have become increasingly important, especially in the wake of the COVID-19 pandemic. These tools enable us to maintain face-to-face interactions with clients, even when in-person meetings are not possible. Virtual meetings can be just as effective as in-person ones for building rapport and trust, provided we use them effectively.

Case Studies: Success Through Relationships

Case Study 1: The Long-term Client

One of my long-term clients, Mr P, is an excellent example of how building strong relationships can lead to sustained success. I first met Mr P over a decade ago when he was looking for a life insurance policy. Through regular interactions and consistent service, our relationship grew beyond the typical advisor-client dynamic.

Over the years, I've assisted Mr P with various insurance and investment needs, and he has referred numerous friends and family members to me. This referral network has been incredibly valuable, significantly expanding my client base. Mr P's trust and confidence in my services have been a testament to the importance of nurturing client relationships over the long term.

Case Study 2: The Corporate Client

In 2015, I began working with a medium-sized company, XYZ Corp., to manage their employee benefits programme. Initially, the relationship was purely transactional. However, by investing time in understanding their specific needs and providing tailored solutions, I was able to build a strong rapport with their HR team and senior management.

This relationship has proven to be mutually beneficial. XYZ Corp. has seen improved employee satisfaction and retention rates due to the comprehensive benefits package we designed. In turn, their positive experience has led to referrals to other businesses within their network, further enhancing my reputation and client base.

Case Study 3: The High-net-worth Individual

Another notable example is my work with Ms T, a high-net-worth individual with complex insurance and investment needs. Building trust with Ms T required a high level of expertise and personalised service. By consistently delivering on these fronts, I was able to establish a strong and lasting relationship.

Ms T's satisfaction with my services has resulted in multiple referrals to her affluent friends and colleagues. These referrals have not only increased my business but also positioned me as a trusted advisor within this exclusive network.

The Future of Relationship Building in Insurance

As we look to the future, the importance of building and maintaining relationships in the insurance profession will only continue to grow. Clients are increasingly seeking advisors who offer personalised service, understand their unique needs, and provide reliable support. By focusing on relationship building, we can differentiate ourselves from competitors and achieve long-term success.

Conclusion

The success of an insurance advisor is intricately linked to the quality of relationships forged. Whether it's leveraging personal connections, going the extra mile for clients, or fostering positive relationships with colleagues and competitors, the power of relationships cannot be overstated. The insurance profession thrives on trust, and trust is built through meaningful, genuine connections.

As advisors, investing time and effort in cultivating these relationships is not just a business strategy but a pathway to long-term success. By

Dr Sijo C. Mathews HC

embracing the symbiotic dance of relationships and business success, we can build bridges that not only sustain but also propel our careers to new heights.

158

Chapter 13
We Don't Close a Sale
Ali Arayssi

Ali Arayssi was born into a business-oriented family in the oriental sweets industry, an upbringing that shaped his entrepreneurial spirit. His international career began in Africa, where he worked in Ghana, Angola, and South Africa, building relationships with traders, merchants, and multinational companies. These experiences taught him the value of communication, cultural sensitivity, and adaptability, alongside the importance of self-reliance and pragmatic decision-making.

In 2015, after returning to Lebanon, Ali unintentionally applied to an insurance company, intending it to be a temporary role. However, over the past nine years, insurance has proven to be the ideal field for him to channel his skills in communication and cultural understanding. Now approaching his sixth MDRT membership, Ali's career reflects his belief that resilience, empathy, and adaptability are essential for achieving success.

His journey is a testament to how challenges and unexpected opportunities can shape a fulfilling and impactful career.

Positive Inner Communication

This chapter will focus on the importance of positive inner communication and the shift from negative language to positive cognition.

What would usually be the first question that your unit/agency/sales manager asks you when you return from a meeting? Did you close the deal? Did you close the sale?

What would your wife or partner ask you when you return from the sales meeting that you have been talking about for days and days and kept telling her:

"Darling, I am busy preparing for that big sales meeting."

"Honey! Did you close?"

While I was preparing for my first post-COVID trip to Dubai, and with all the financial hardships and economic crises in Lebanon, my country, I asked myself what the first question I would answer after every scheduled meeting would be: *Did I close?*

This is when it hit me—in the shower, which is where all great ideas usually come to us. I asked myself why it is called closing.

The Meaning of Closing

The word *"close"* or *"closing,"* by definition, means:

- to end something
- to terminate access to a computer file or program
- to conclude a discussion or negotiation
- to perform something previously agreed to, such as closing a real estate title transfer

The adjective of the word *"closing"* means bringing something to an end—finality.

The Science of Negative Language

When we use negative words, we're keeping certain neurochemicals from being produced, which contributes to stress management. As humans, we're hardwired to worry; it's how our primal brain protects us from dangerous situations for survival. So, when we allow negative words and concepts into our thoughts, we increase the activity in our brain's fear centre, causing stress-producing hormones to flood our system. These hormones and neurotransmitters interrupt the logic and reasoning processes in the brain, and inhibit normal functionality.

Newberg and Waldman write:

> *"Angry words send alarm messages through the brain, and they partially shut down the logic and reasoning centres in the frontal lobes."*

Another scientific explanation is that our brain's fear centre, the amygdala, gets activated when we encounter negative words or phrases. This triggers the release of stress hormones, including cortisol, preparing our body for a fight-or-flight response. Constant exposure to negativity can lead to chronic stress, impairing cognitive function and decision-making.

The Impact of Negative Language on Thinking

1. **Self-doubt and limiting beliefs:** Constant exposure to negative words can cultivate self-doubt and foster limiting beliefs. When we repeatedly hear phrases like "impossible", "can't", or "failure", our subconscious absorbs these messages, influencing our perception of our capabilities and potential.
2. **Pessimism and outlook:** Negative words contribute to a pessimistic outlook. When our language is infused with negativity, we tend to focus on problems rather than solutions. This pessimism can hinder our ability to see opportunities and impede creative thinking.
3. **Increased stress and anxiety:** The stress response triggered by negative words contributes to heightened levels of stress and anxiety. Chronic exposure to stress hormones can have detrimental effects on mental health, leading to increased anxiety, difficulty concentrating, and a diminished ability to cope with challenges.
4. **Resistance to change:** Negative words often create resistance to change. Phrases like "it won't work" or "it's too difficult" instil a mindset resistant to innovation and adaptation. This resistance can impede personal and professional growth.
5. **Impact on relationships:** Negative words can strain relationships. Constantly using critical or pessimistic language can create a hostile environment, leading to

misunderstandings, conflicts, and strained connections with others.

The Power of Positive Cognition

Cognitive scientists continue to explore how the brain processes negative versus positive sentence structures. Positive self-talk can kick-start a neural chain reaction that motivates you to succeed.

So, why should you wire your brain with a negative word? Why should you worry about a meeting before you even go there?

When you first sit with a prospect, are you planning to close a deal?

From Closing to Opening

Think about it: that's what you have been told day after day, year after year, in each training course, in each book, in each sales technique, but the truth is you should not be aiming to close; you should be aiming to open.

The purpose of every meeting is to open the doors to a long-term relationship with the prospect, a relationship based on knowing each other, understanding their aims and dreams, and trust.

That's the purpose of every meeting, irrelevant of the immediate direct result; that meeting might open the door to a business relationship, multiple deals, referrals, and perhaps friendship.

Ali Arayssi

The Dynamics of Client Relationships in Sales

In the dynamic realm of sales, where transactions often extend beyond mere business exchanges, the significance of positive client relationships cannot be overstated. Building and maintaining strong connections with clients goes far beyond closing a deal; it lays the foundation for enduring success and mutual growth.

What are the Dynamics of Client Relationships in Sales?

1. **The human element:** Sales are fundamentally human interactions. Behind every transaction is a person with needs, aspirations, and concerns. Recognising and valuing this human element is the cornerstone of building positive client relationships.
2. **Trust as the bedrock:** Trust is the currency of successful client relationships. Clients who trust the sales professional are more likely to engage in long-term partnerships. Trust is earned through transparent communication, reliability, and a genuine commitment to the client's best interests.
3. **Beyond the transaction:** A positive client relationship extends beyond the confines of a single transaction. It involves understanding the client's goals, challenges, and professional landscape. This holistic approach enhances the sales process and positions the sales professional as a trusted advisor.

The Impact of Positive Client Relationships on Sales Professionals

1. **Enhanced credibility and authority:** Positive client relationships elevate sales professionals' credibility. When

clients perceive the salesperson as a trustworthy advisor, it lends authority to recommendations and proposals. This enhanced credibility facilitates smoother negotiations and leads to a higher conversion rate.

2. **Repeat business and customer loyalty:** Satisfied clients are more likely to return for future business. Positive client relationships foster customer loyalty, reducing the need for constant prospecting. Repeat business not only boosts sales revenue but also contributes to the growth and stability of the sales professional's portfolio.

3. **Referrals as a testimony:** A happy client is a powerful advocate. Positive relationships lead to satisfied clients who are often willing to provide referrals. Word-of-mouth recommendations carry substantial weight in business and can open doors to new opportunities and clientele.

4. **Resilience in challenging times:** Positive client relationships act as a buffer when faced with challenges or setbacks. Clients with a positive rapport with their sales professionals are more likely to be understanding and collaborative during tough times, fostering resilience in the face of adversity.

Strategies for Building and Nurturing Positive Client Relationships

1. **Active listening:** Active listening is the foundation of any positive relationship. Sales professionals should prioritise understanding the client's needs, concerns, and objectives. This demonstrates empathy and allows for tailored solutions that address the client's specific challenges.

2. **Open and transparent communication:** Transparency is key to building trust. Sales professionals should communicate

openly about product offerings, pricing structures, and potential challenges. This transparency builds credibility and reassures clients that they are making informed decisions.

3. **Personalised service:** Clients appreciate a personalised approach. Understanding their unique preferences, professional nuances, and communication styles allows sales professionals to tailor their interactions and offerings. This personalised touch goes a long way in building a positive client experience.

4. **Timely and reliable follow-ups:** Consistent and reliable follow-ups are a hallmark of positive client relationships. Whether post-sale support or routine check-ins, timely communication reinforces the client's value and demonstrates the sales professional's commitment to their success.

5. **Anticipating client needs:** Proactively anticipating client needs showcases foresight and commitment. Sales professionals who go beyond reactive problem-solving to foresee challenges and propose solutions position themselves as indispensable partners in their clients' journeys.

6. **Building emotional intelligence:** Understanding and managing emotions, both one's own and the client's, is crucial in sales. Emotional intelligence enables sales professionals to navigate delicate situations, build rapport, and respond empathetically to client concerns.

The Ripple Effect: Positive Client Relationships Beyond Sales

1. **Brand advocacy:** Positive client relationships extend beyond individual sales professionals to impact the broader brand. Satisfied clients often become brand advocates, promoting

products and services within their professional networks and circles. They essentially become your marketer and promoter.

2. **Positive organisational image:** Sales professionals are ambassadors of their organisations. Positive client relationships contribute to an overall positive image of the organisation. This positive perception can attract new clients, partners, and top talent to the company.

3. **Long-term partnerships:** Organisations thrive when they establish long-term partnerships with clients. Positive client relationships are the bedrock of enduring collaborations, fostering a sense of loyalty and partnership that goes beyond individual transactions.

How do we Measure Positive Client Relationships?

1. **Client satisfaction surveys:** Regular client satisfaction surveys provide valuable insights into the client's experience. These surveys can gauge satisfaction levels, identify areas for improvement, and highlight specific strengths in the client-professional relationship.

2. **Client retention rates:** High client retention rates indicate positive client relationships. Monitoring retention rates over time can help assess the strength of client relationships and the effectiveness of the strategies employed.

3. **Referral rates:** The number of referrals from existing clients is a tangible measure of satisfaction. A high rate of client referrals suggests a positive reputation and the likelihood of attracting new business through word of mouth.

Ali Arayssi

A Lesson in Building Relationships: Ghana

All of these ideas and concepts took me back to 2001 when I first travelled to Ghana, Africa. It was my first work trip outside of Lebanon. I had zero knowledge of Ghana, its culture, habits, and people. I was handling sales for a powdered milk company, and I was supposed to introduce the product to a highly competitive market.

The market is run by *"mamas"*—Ghanaian women who manage businesses while their husbands work in the public or private sector. So, imagine me; a newcomer who didn't speak the local language and didn't know the culture; and for them, I was the *"obroni"*—the white man.

It was hard; there were many rejections and closed doors, and the strategy of using distributors seemed to fail. I then did what I thought was the best option—to go and meet the merchants directly. I used to drive all over the country, stop at every shop, and meet every shop owner and mama on my way. I would walk through markets and talk to mamas or owners.

Over time, I got to know everyone—from Wa to Takoradi and from Tamale to Tema—travelling as far north as the jungle and to the borders of Côte d'Ivoire and Togo. The business grew from selling strips to boxes to containers—20-foot containers.

When I reflected on this during my Dubai trip, I realised that my success in Ghana was not about the product but about *me*. The relationships I built with the people there; understanding their likes and dislikes, and sharing *fufu*, the traditional dish, with them, was the secret to success. I opened a relationship with them; I never went to close a deal or a sale.

It certainly took time, sweat, and perhaps some losses in the beginning. Still, it taught me a lesson that I carry in my advisory business today: create a relationship with your client and make them your friend. Don't take *"obroni"* as a bad word; take it as a friendly term from people who appreciate your friendship.

Shifting Focus: Opening Instead of Closing

What would the impact be if your unit/agency/sales managers, or even your wives or partners, asked you: *Did you open the deal? Did you open the meeting?*

Sounds silly?

I am shifting my words from negative to positive; I won't worry about closing anymore. I will enjoy opening a new relationship.

Words are more than just communication instruments; they are creators of our ideas and mindsets. Negative language profoundly affects our thoughts, leading to tension, pessimism, and self-doubt. Conversely, positive language has the transformative ability to improve resilience, self-assurance, and general well-being.

As we manoeuvre through the complex fabric of our everyday existence, let us be designers of hope. By making thoughtful language choices, we may transform our thoughts, develop a positive outlook, and set out on a path to a happier and more fulfilled life.

Conclusion: Build Relationships not Sales

If there is one lesson to summarise, it is this: we are in the profession of people, and people are susceptible to approaches. Stop being a salesperson and become a relationship builder—it's a win-win situation.

Ali Arayssi

Notes:

Change your Words and Change Your Brain – for the Better, an article in *Arkadin Magazine.*

Choosing Positive Words Improves Mindset and Performance, cognitive scientists confirm the power of affirmative language. Published December 7th, 2012.

Part Five
Advanced Strategies and Adaptability

Chapter 14
Closing Big Deals in Thirty Minutes
Miliana Marten

Miliana Marten, CFP®, AEPP®, is a financial planner with an internationally recognised CFP® (Certified Financial Planner) certification, and has been a member of MDRT (Million Dollar Round Table) since 2010.

She is a qualifying and honour roll MDRT member with 16 years of MDRT membership, including 8 Court of the Table and 2 Top of the Table qualifications. Having been a university lecturer for 8 years before joining the profession in 2004, Miliana, along with her husband, established MD Academy and MD Team to train individuals seeking greater success in their careers. She served as Country Chair for MDRT Indonesia from 2019 to 2021.

As a thyroid cancer survivor, she has a strong belief in the insurance profession and the miracle of insurance products. Her passion lies in helping people protect their lives financially, especially in legacy planning and charitable giving.

The Impact of the Pandemic on the Insurance Profession

The pandemic that started in 2019 brought significant changes to the insurance profession. Previously, a financial planner had to meet prospective customers face to face, in order to make sales. However, during the pandemic, the government allowed virtual transactions, eliminating the need for in-person meetings. All transactions could be completed with e-signatures, which significantly streamlined the process.

These changing conditions made the performance of a financial planner more efficient. There was no longer the need to waste time travelling to meet potential customers, and there were no more parking fees, toll fees, or entertainment costs involved in closing a deal. The time saved could be used to reach more clients, thus increasing productivity and potential sales.

In 2021, while the pandemic was still ongoing, I made substantial sales by conducting a virtual presentation in just 30 minutes, which helped me reach the Top of the Table. This achievement highlighted the potential of virtual meetings for closing big deals efficiently.

Several tips can help insurance professionals close deals in 30 minutes. These can be summarised into three parts:

1. Have the Right Mindset

It is crucial to understand that many people still need insurance. Financial planners often find it challenging to make insurance sales, especially big-case sales, because they think many people already have insurance, don't want more, or don't have the budget. However, the pandemic made people more aware of the importance of having insurance protection.

Recognising Market Potential

In the Asian market, particularly in Indonesia, insurance literacy remains very low. This is an excellent time for financial planners to reach out to those without insurance and those who are underinsured, as the opportunity for upselling is significant.

The pandemic has highlighted vulnerabilities that many individuals had not previously considered. Health scares, job losses, and economic uncertainties underscored the necessity of having a safety net. This realisation created a more receptive audience for insurance products.

Financial planners need to understand that while many people may already have some form of insurance, they might not have adequate coverage. This opens a vast market for upselling additional coverage or new policies tailored to current needs.

The Story of High-net-worth Cases in 2021

During the pandemic, when the infection rate was still relatively high, I managed to reach the Top of the Table (TOT) with a target six times bigger than MDRT.

In 2020, many people experienced a decrease in income. Many office workers faced salary adjustments or had their work contracts suspended. Businesses struggled because they had to pay employee salaries while turnover decreased.

In difficult times like these, when most people thought business was plummeting and income was falling, was there still anyone willing to buy big insurance?

I was fortunate to have a mentor, Solomon Hicks, who encouraged me and instilled the mindset in me that reaching the Top of the Table was entirely achievable.

In fact, during the pandemic, certain business sectors saw their performance skyrocket, such as the pharmaceutical and technology industries At that time, everyone needed masks, vitamins, vaccines, medicines, oxygen cylinders, and other medical supplies. These became essential needs. This mindset motivated me to step out of my comfort zone and believe that people genuinely needed insurance protection.

Adapting to Virtual Sales

The pandemic proved that insurance sales could be conducted virtually. This method allowed financial planners to reach prospects not only in their city but in other cities as well. Many financial planners still believe that meeting potential customers face to face is necessary to convince them. However, even in 2025, long after the pandemic ended, I still meet potential customers virtually.

Virtual Meetings and Webinars

Virtual meetings, such as webinars, can be conducted one-on-one or in larger groups. I typically conduct one-on-one virtual meetings via Zoom for 30 minutes. When requesting an appointment with a prospective customer, I ask for 30 minutes to discuss their needs. This approach usually secures the appointment.

Mass virtual meetings, like webinars, are also effective. During the pandemic, I held webinars almost monthly. These regular webinars engaged customers and prospective clients, giving them the impression that I am an expert in financial planning. Although I hold webinars less frequently now, in 2025, they remain an essential part of my strategy.

Leveraging Technology

Embracing technology is crucial. Tools like Zoom, Microsoft Teams, and Google Meet allow financial planners to schedule and conduct meetings seamlessly. Additionally, platforms that support digital document signing, such as DocuSign, have made the transaction process smoother. These tools save time and make the process more convenient for clients, thereby increasing the likelihood of closing deals quickly.

2. Trust and Branding

The most crucial element in sales is potential customers' trust in their financial planner. Trust encourages clients to open their network and introduce their financial planner to others.

Building Personal Branding

Personal branding is essential for creating a memorable identity that clients and potential prospects can easily remember. Authenticity is key to successful personal branding. As my background includes being a university lecturer, I frequently post on social media about providing financial planning education to prospective customers and other financial planners.

Being invited to speak nationally and internationally helped establish my reputation as an expert in the insurance profession. I created branding on multiple social media platforms, including Instagram, Facebook, LinkedIn, a personal website, YouTube, and TikTok. A 360-

degree marketing approach incorporating online and offline branding helps increase client trust.

Establishing Expertise

Creating content that demonstrates expertise is vital. Writing articles, making videos, and participating in professional discussions on platforms like LinkedIn can position a financial planner as a thought leader. Clients who perceive you as knowledgeable and credible are more likely to trust your advice and refer you to others.

I received a WhatsApp message some time back from my client, Mr James, who is the CEO of a big company. He introduced me to his friend, Mr Budi, who was seeking insurance. To prepare, I conducted a fact-finding mission about Mr Budi by searching his name on Google and checking his social media profiles. This research revealed that Mr Budi was a successful young entrepreneur in the pharmaceutical sector; an American university graduate under 40 years old, with two young children.

I contacted Mr Budi and introduced myself, asking for a 30-minute appointment. Here's how our conversation went:

> *"Hello Mr Budi; let me introduce myself. I am Miliana, a financial planner from XXX Company. Mr James informed me you were seeking information about family financial planning. I would be happy to help. [Link to my LinkedIn profile: https://www.linkedin.com/in/milianamarten.]"*

Mr Budi responded positively but mentioned his busy schedule. I suggested a 30-minute Zoom meeting, which he agreed to.

3. It Only Takes 30 Minutes

Financial planners must train themselves in simple and effective presentation techniques that can be delivered to prospects quickly.

Preparing for the Meeting

Preparation is vital for making the most of a 30-minute meeting. Before the meeting, gather all relevant information about the prospect. Understand their financial status, needs, and potential concerns. This preparation allows you to effectively tailor your presentation to address their specific situation.

Conducting the Meeting

As promised, I needed to use all of those 30 minutes for the discussion with Mr Budi, who was very punctual. Five minutes before 5 o'clock, I opened my Zoom room. Precisely at 5 o'clock, he entered the Zoom meeting.

As an icebreaker, I opened the initial conversation with a chat about our mutual friend, Mr James. I told him about how Mr James had introduced him to me.

After the icebreaker, I asked, *"What made you interested in learning more about financial planning?"*

"I already have a lot of insurance, but after I checked my nominal amount, it's not enough considering my current condition," Mr Budi explained. *"The last time I bought insurance was five years ago, with a guaranteed sum assured of USD 300,000,"* he continued.

Mr Budi wanted to increase the protection value of his insurance, as he considered the current protection too small. Based on this information, a financial planner would need to develop an income protection programme that suits their needs.

Considering that Mr Budi is still young, his wife is a housewife, and they have two small children, the income protection calculation required—especially after the policyholder dies or becomes critically ill —is five times the annual income.

Explaining the Benefits

Why should it be five times the annual income? This protection is required for the following expenses:

- **Immediate expenses:** Expenses that must be paid immediately, such as final expenses upon death, tax debt, credit card debt, and others.
- **Ongoing expenses:** Expenses that will continue, such as living expenses for the spouse, children's school fees, and others.
- **Future expenses:** Expenditures to achieve future dreams, such as children's education, future needs, and other goals.

Presentations are more effective when accompanied by stories. You can use your customer's claim story or someone else's claim story. In this case, I shared my own claim story, explaining how insurance protected me financially when I had to survive thyroid cancer, which I was diagnosed with in 2017. I was fortunate that my hospital bills were fully covered, and I received a significant critical illness claim. For me, I truly experienced the miracle of insurance in my life.

Closing the Deal

After listening to the presentation and claim story, Mr Budi asked me to calculate an insurance proposal with a guaranteed sum assured of USD 3,000,000 and critical illness insurance with a guaranteed sum assured of USD 1,000,000.

Because I had practised and prepared calculation simulations beforehand, I could calculate the amounts quickly, and immediately explain the proposals for the life insurance and critical illness insurance programmes.

Even though there were no objections, Mr Budi still wanted to consider the offer. The 30-minute meeting ended there, and I asked for a follow-up meeting the following week.

After being delayed for three weeks due to his busy schedule, we finally had another opportunity to meet via Zoom for another 30 minutes. In this second meeting, Mr Budi decided to buy life insurance with a guaranteed sum assured of USD 3,000,000 and critical illness insurance with a guaranteed sum assured of USD 1,000,000. Meanwhile, for his wife, a housewife, critical illness insurance was purchased with a guaranteed sum assured of USD 1,000,000.

Efficient Transaction Process

During the pandemic, the insurance purchase transaction process became more accessible. All insurance applications could be done online and did not require face-to-face contact.

With a large sum assured, a medical check-up is, of course, required. Before the pandemic, I usually had to accompany clients to the medical check-up. During the pandemic, insurance companies provided a mobile doctor panel service where the medical personnel visited the client's house.

After the medical examination was complete, the financial underwriting process was carried out. The trust between financial planners and clients made clients very cooperative in completing the required documents, such as account books for the last six months and a list of assets.

All processes ran smoothly—from applying for insurance, the medical check-up, and the underwriting process, where the offer to reinsurance was made, until the policy was finally issued. It took less than one month.

After completing all the processes and issuing the policy, I automatically achieved TOT (Top of the Table) status.

Lessons Learned

- Big cases can close even if the meetings are online.
- The success of closing big deals online proves that virtual meetings can be just as effective as in-person meetings.
- Big cases can be obtained through referrals from other customers. Building trust and maintaining good relationships is crucial.
- Big cases do not always undergo a complicated and lengthy process. Efficient processes and good preparation can streamline the sales process.

Conclusion

Financial planners can close significant deals efficiently by embracing virtual sales, maintaining a solid personal brand, and building trust with clients. The pandemic reshaped the insurance profession, offering new opportunities for adaptable, forward-thinking individuals.

The ability to close big deals in just 30 minutes requires a combination of the right mindset, effective use of technology, solid personal branding, and the ability to build trust quickly. These elements, when combined, can lead to significant achievements in the financial planning profession. As we move forward, the lessons learned during the pandemic will continue to shape how we conduct business, making us more efficient and effective in reaching and serving our clients.

Chapter 15
Golden Number 10950
John Fernandes

John Fernandes is a seasoned financial planner with over 22 years of experience, serving more than 3,200 families in achieving their financial goals. Based in Mumbai, India, John leads a successful practice founded on integrity, personalised service, and expert guidance. His firm offers a range of services, including life insurance, mutual funds, fixed deposits, and health insurance, ensuring his clients' financial security.

John holds an MBA in insurance and financial planning from Chitkara University and a Master's degree in finance from Mumbai University, both earned with first-class distinctions. Before starting his practice, he gained experience in sales, accounting, and income tax as an assistant manager at Mettler Toledo India Pvt Ltd, laying the foundation for his client-focused approach.

Passionate about empowering families to live with confidence, John combines professionalism and personalised solutions to deliver impactful financial guidance. His dedication continues to leave a lasting legacy in the financial planning profession.

Introduction:

10950: The Golden Number for Retirement

Retirement offers a huge opportunity to pursue activities that can't be achieved during an active work life. It's a second phase where one can enjoy hobbies, travel to different countries, or spend quality time with family members. This phase is about enjoying the fruits of the hard work that was done during your professional years.

Retirement can also bring about significant lifestyle changes, such as relocating to areas that suit one's preferences, downsizing to a smaller home, moving closer to family, or seeking a new climate or community.

Retirement doesn't mean the end of learning. Many retirees enjoy taking classes, attending workshops, or pursuing educational opportunities that they didn't have time for earlier in life. This period also offers the chance to relax and enjoy life without work pressures. Whether reading a book, indulging in hobbies, or simply soaking in the beauty of nature, retirees often savour the slower pace of retirement life.

Everyone wishes for a fruitful retirement, but not everyone effectively plans for it. Successful retirement requires careful financial planning, health management, and adjustments to lifestyles and routines. Ultimately, retirement offers an opportunity for reflection, fulfilment, and enjoying the fruits of one's labour. Balancing leisure and meaningful activities is vital to maximising the retirement years.

Financial stability is one of the critical aspects of retirement, and it ensures that you are not dependent on charities or forced to work during your retirement. In India, retirement life is also called the "second innings" of life, which depends on the first innings. In many countries, the government takes care of their employees during retirement, so they don't need to plan extensively for retirement. In India, only government employees are blessed with the government taking care of them in their old age. However, this is changing due to the heavy cost on the government treasury.

As said, finance is all about numbers, and many clients find it difficult to manage these numbers. So, we came up with a simple solution—just remember **10950**. This is your retirement number.

We also randomly ask prospects about this number, which keeps them thinking and makes them curious to know what it means. Often, they will call us and request an appointment to meet them and explain in detail. This question allows us to talk at length, and the best part is that clients give us their undivided attention. The number **10950** has helped to open many doors that would not have opened without it.

10950 - What's this Number?

Is it a lotto number? A lottery game number? A lucky number? No, it's your retirement number for yourself and your spouse.

10950 is the number of meals you'll consume from the age of 60 to 70 (3 meals per day); 3 x 365 = 1095 meals per year. Hence, for ten years, that will equal 10950 meals.

So, if three meals cost $10 per day, you will need 10950 x 10, which equals $109,500. This simple calculation shows how much money you will need for your food expenses without accounting for other costs, and this is only for one person.

To enjoy a comfortable retirement life for yourself and your spouse, you will need discipline and commitment to save regularly. Many products are available to help you plan your retirement, but the best ones are life insurance annuity plans or life insurance retirement plans.

Why Life Insurance Annuities?

Clients often ask why they should choose life insurance annuity plans over other products like mutual funds, fixed deposits, or rental income. The answer is simple: once someone starts a life insurance annuity plan, it forces them to save, and does not allow them to withdraw the funds before they turn 60. All other products in the market give clients the option to exit whenever they wish, and many times, this becomes a stumbling block for retirement plans, due to their impatience.

I met Mr Anand through one of my existing clients, who had purchased a life insurance annuity and referred him to me. Anand completed his MBA in sales marketing and worked in the telecommunications industry. Despite being referred by my existing client, getting an appointment with him was difficult. He was married, and his spouse worked in the media industry. Both were busy professionals with demanding jobs and handsome salaries.

After fact-finding and understanding their risk profile, we decided on a $100,000 annuity plan, which would increase by 10% every two years to beat inflation and allow them to manage their lifestyle accordingly. Everything was going well until COVID-19 struck, and Anand lost his job. He was forced to withdraw all of his investments except for the life insurance annuities. He did not pay premiums for a couple of years, but in September 2023, he revived his policy by paying all of the missed instalments. He was then back on track to receive an annuity on the $100,000 premium.

In my 22 years of experience in this field, I have witnessed many individuals like Anand liquidate their investments due to fear of the market, to book profit, or to enjoy their current life. Life insurance annuities are the only product that people hold onto until they retire, or rather, they are forced to do so.

Planning for Longevity

In India, the average life expectancy is around 71 to 75 years, but in European and other countries, this number is higher. Hence, for a non-resident Indian or a foreign national of Indian origin, we double the number **10950.**

Even after addressing all objections raised by the client, if they still do not agree, we suggest taking an annuity plan for their spouse as a gift from them. This way, even if they are not around in old age, the company will pay the annuity in their name. This can be the best retirement gift for a spouse.

I remember a client from the defence world who, may his soul rest in peace, initially objected to buying an annuity plan because the government provided him with a substantial pension. However, he liked the idea of providing an annuity for his wife and took the plan for $50,000. After seven years, he died in the Kargil War, but his wife continued to receive the annuity he had provided for her.

Life insurance annuities, or the number **10950,** give you and your spouse the freedom to achieve all those things in your second innings that you missed during your prime working years. It provides freedom from dependence on children or charities, and ensures self-respect for you and your spouse. Passive or annuity income is much better than relying on amounts received from others.

Beyond Basic Needs

The figure **10950** is just a starting point. While it covers the necessity of food, a comprehensive retirement plan must also account for other expenses such as healthcare, housing, travel, and leisure activities.

Healthcare can become a significant expense as we age. A robust healthcare plan alongside your annuities can safeguard against unexpected medical costs, ensuring that your savings are not depleted due to unforeseen health issues.

The Role of Annuities in Estate Planning

Annuities can also play a crucial role in estate planning. They can be structured to provide a steady income stream to your beneficiaries after your demise, ensuring that your legacy continues to support your loved ones. This feature is particularly beneficial for those who wish to leave a financial safety net for their spouses or children.

Estate planning with annuities involves setting up the annuity contracts to continue to pay out even after the policyholder's death. This can be a significant advantage over other investment options that might not offer the same level of security and predictability.

Inflation Protection

One of the biggest concerns in retirement planning is inflation. The cost of living continues to rise, and what seems like an adequate amount today might not be sufficient in the future.

Annuities that offer inflation protection can adjust the payout amounts to keep up with the increasing costs, ensuring that your purchasing power remains intact. Inflation-protected annuities typically come with a cost, but their peace of mind can be invaluable. By opting for such plans, retirees can ensure that their income keeps pace with inflation, protecting their lifestyle and financial independence.

The Psychological Benefits of Annuities

Beyond the financial advantages, annuities also offer psychological benefits. Knowing that you have a guaranteed income for life can reduce stress and anxiety about outliving your savings. This sense of financial security allows retirees to enjoy their retirement years more fully, focusing on activities they love rather than worrying about money.

The predictable income stream from annuities can also help with budgeting and financial planning. By knowing exactly how much money they will receive each month, retirees can plan their expenses more effectively.

Customising your Annuity Plan

Annuities are not a one-size-fits-all solution. They can be customised to meet individual needs and preferences. For instance, some might prefer a higher initial payout that decreases over time, while others might opt for a level payout that remains consistent throughout retirement.

Customising your annuity plan involves considering various factors such as your health, life expectancy, and financial goals. Working with a financial advisor can help you choose the best annuity structure that aligns with your retirement objectives.

Combining Annuities with Other Investments

While annuities are a powerful tool for retirement planning, they should not be the sole component of your retirement portfolio. Diversifying your investments can help spread risk and increase potential returns.

Combining annuities with other investment options, such as stocks, bonds, and mutual funds, can create a balanced and robust retirement plan. Diversification ensures that you are not overly dependent on a single source of income. It provides flexibility and potential growth, complementing the stability offered by annuities.

Case Studies: Success Stories with Annuities

Over the years, I have witnessed numerous success stories where annuities have provided retirees with financial security and peace of mind. Let me share a few:

Case Study 1:

Mr and Mrs Sharma approached me with concerns about their retirement savings. They had a substantial amount saved but were worried about market volatility affecting their investments. We set up a series of annuities for them, ensuring a guaranteed income stream. Despite market fluctuations, they have enjoyed a stable income and have been able to travel extensively during their retirement.

Case Study 2:

Mrs Patel, a single retiree, was concerned about outliving her savings. She opted for a lifetime annuity with inflation protection. This has provided her with financial stability and allowed her to focus on her hobbies and volunteer work without worrying about her finances.

John Fernandes

Case Study 3:

Mr Reddy, a business owner, wanted to ensure his wife would be financially secure after his death. He set up a joint-life annuity that continues to pay out to his wife after his passing. This decision has provided Mr Reddy and his wife immense peace of mind.

Conclusion: The Freedom of 10950

The number **10950** is more than just a calculation; it represents the freedom and security of proper retirement planning. By understanding and implementing the concept of **10950**, retirees can ensure they have enough funds to cover their basic needs and enjoy their retirement without financial worries.

Life insurance annuities provide a disciplined approach to retirement savings, protecting against market volatility and ensuring a steady income stream. They offer a comprehensive solution to retirement planning, addressing financial needs and providing psychological and emotional benefits.

Retirement is a time to enjoy the fruits of your labour, pursue your passions, and spend time with loved ones. With proper planning and the right financial tools, you can make your retirement years truly golden.

Remember, the key to a successful retirement lies in understanding your needs, planning, and choosing the right financial products that align with your goals. And sometimes, all it takes is a simple number —**10950**—to set you on the right path.

By making informed decisions and staying committed to your retirement plan, you can achieve financial independence and enjoy a fulfilling retirement. So, start planning today, and let the golden number **10950** guide you towards a secure and happy retirement.

Chapter 16
Adapt and Fly
Panos Leledakis

Panos Leledakis brings 25 years of expertise in insurance and financial planning, earning recognition as a top awarded consultant and TOT MDRT member since 1999. Known as a pioneer and futurist in the insurance industry, he specialises in digital transformation, artificial intelligence, internet marketing strategies, automation, and emerging technologies such as virtual and augmented reality.

Panos is the inventor of two innovative software solutions for insurance needs analyses and financial planning, integrating artificial intelligence, neuroscience, and behavioural economics. His groundbreaking work has earned him 11 global innovation awards, including honours from MIT.

He holds a certification in "AI for Business" from the University of Pennsylvania and is pursuing advanced AI studies at MIT. Manos also holds LUTCF, IRMA, and BRMA certifications and is furthering his expertise with PRMIA. In 2020, he was named one of the "Top 25 InsurTech CEOs of 2020."

A dynamic public speaker, Panos has inspired audiences in over 45 countries with his motivational style.

Embracing Technology in Insurance and Financial Planning

In the fast-paced world of insurance and financial planning, adapting and embracing new technologies can make the difference between success and stagnation. This chapter explores how advisors can leverage cutting-edge tools to create unforgettable digital experiences for their clients, starting with the inspiring journey of one advisor who turned adversity into opportunity through technology.

A Journey of Necessity and Innovation

Panos Leledakis started his career in the insurance industry in 1999, full of enthusiasm and ready to make his mark. However, fate had other plans. Just nine months into his new profession, tragedy struck—his father passed away, leaving behind a substantial inheritance tax bill. Determined to overcome this financial hurdle, Panos sought advice from an MDRT member, who suggested a seemingly impossible solution: conduct five appointments per day to generate the necessary commissions.

Living in Athens, Greece, at the time, Panos quickly realised that the city's notorious traffic made this goal nearly unattainable through traditional face-to-face meetings. Then, he had his eureka moment—why not use Skype, the emerging video calling technology, to meet with clients virtually?

This innovative approach wasn't without its challenges. Convincing clients to embrace this new method of communication and training them to use the technology required patience and persistence. But Panos's efforts paid off handsomely. By saving countless hours previously lost to commuting, he met his financial goals and discovered a passion for technology that would shape the rest of his career.

From then on, Panos fell in love with technology and made it his mission to be at the forefront of technological adoption in the insurance industry. He began prospecting and recruiting through webinars as early as 2010, a practice far from common at the time. By 2015, he had transformed his entire practice into a digital operation.

Creating Unforgettable Digital First Impressions

As Panos often says, *"You never get a second chance to create an amazing first digital experience."* In today's world, where virtual meetings have become the norm, standing out from the crowd is more crucial than ever. Let's explore how insurance and financial planning advisors can elevate their digital presence and create memorable client experiences.

The Power of the Right Equipment

1. **High-quality webcam**: Invest in a webcam that offers crisp, clear video. The Logitech C920, for instance, provides excellent 1080p resolution at an affordable price point. Remember that your image is often the first thing clients see— make it count!

2. **Green screen and OBS**: A green screen backdrop, coupled with the free software OBS or the paid Ecamm, allows you to replace your background with professional looking virtual sets. This not only looks impressive but also helps maintain client privacy by hiding your actual surroundings.

3. **Stream deck**: This nifty device lets you automate various actions with the push of a button. Change scenes, play videos, or share your screen seamlessly without interrupting your presentation flow. It's like having a personal production assistant at your fingertips!

Sound: The Unsung Hero of Virtual Meetings

As Panos emphasises, sound quality accounts for 70% of a presentation's success. Here are some options to ensure your audio is crystal clear:

1. **Lavalier microphone**: For a budget-friendly option, a simple USB Lavalier microphone can significantly improve your sound quality. It's a small investment that makes a big difference.

2. **Professional USB microphone**: Step up your game with a high-quality USB microphone like the Blue Yeti. These offer studio-grade sound without the complexity of a full audio setup.

3. **Sound console**: For those ready to go the extra mile, a sound console like the Rodecaster Pro opens a world of possibilities. Add sound effects, control multiple audio sources, and achieve that coveted "radio DJ" quality in your voice.

Setting up your Digital Studio

Whether working from a dedicated office or carving out a corner of your home, creating a professional looking space for virtual meetings is crucial. Here's what you need:

1. **Lighting**: Good lighting can make a basic webcam look great. Consider investing in a ring light or softbox to ensure you're always well illuminated.
2. **Backdrop**: A simple, clean backdrop can work wonders if a green screen isn't feasible. A plain wall, tasteful bookshelf, or subtle branded background can all create a professional atmosphere.
3. **Camera placement**: Position your camera at eye level for the most flattering and engaging angle. This might mean propping up your laptop or adjusting your external webcam.

Beyond Meetings: Leveraging your Setup for Content Creation

The beauty of investing in a professional virtual meeting setup is that it serves double duty for content creation. Use the same equipment to:

1. **Record professional videos**: Create high-quality educational content, client testimonials, or product explanations.
2. **Host webinars**: Conduct engaging online seminars to prospect, educate, and build your brand.
3. **Produce podcasts**: Launch an audio show to share your expertise and connect with a broader audience.

The Power of Personal Visibility: Mastering Content Marketing in the Digital Age

By consistently creating valuable content, you'll establish yourself as a thought leader in your field, attracting clients and building trust before you meet.

Content is King (and Queen)!

First things first, let's talk about the types of content you can create:

- Video testimonials from satisfied clients (nothing beats social proof!)
- Informative articles (show off that expertise!)
- Engaging videos (lights, camera, action!)
- Podcasts (because who doesn't love a good listen?)
- Eye-catching infographics (visual learners, rejoice!)
- Valuable eBooks (the ultimate lead magnet!)

I know what you're thinking: *"But Panos, I'm not a professional content creator!"* Well, guess what? You don't need to be! With today's technology, you can become a content creating machine with just your smartphone and a few free tools.

Lights, Camera, Action!

Let's start with video. Your smartphone's camera is probably better than most professional cameras from a few years ago. Pair that with a cheap wireless microphone, and you're golden!

But wait, there's more! Use a free teleprompter app to read your script smoothly, and suddenly, you're the next big thing on YouTube!

Don't even worry about the quality of sound when you record! AI sound enhancers like Adobe Podcast Software can clean that up for you. And for editing? Free software like CapCut has got you covered. You'll be creating Hollywood quality videos in no time!

Design Like a Pro

Now, let's talk design. Canva is your new best friend. This free tool lets you create stunning posts, infographics, and even eBooks. And here's the kicker—Canva now has AI capabilities to help you create bulk content. It's like having a personal design team in your pocket!

The AI Revolution

Speaking of AI, let me tell you—content creation has never been easier than in 2023. Writer's block? A thing of the past! AI can help you create article scripts, video outlines, eBook content, and even podcast questions in minutes. It's like having a team of writers at your fingertips!

But here's the real magic: AI can help you understand your audience better. Target a specific market, ask AI about their concerns and desires, and create content that speaks directly to them. It's like being a mind reader, but better!

Grow that Email List

Now, let's talk about growing your email list. Create a valuable eBook (remember, AI can help with this) and set up a landing page offering it for free in exchange for an email address. Share this in social media groups where your target market hangs out. Before you know it, your email list will grow faster than a teenager in a growth spurt!

From Suspects to Prospects to Clients

Once you have those email addresses, nurture those contacts. Send them valuable content regularly and then invite them to a value-added webinar where you can pitch your practice to hundreds at once. It's like fishing with dynamite—but legal and much more ethical!

The Ultimate Goal

Remember, the goal here is to position yourself as the go-to expert in your field. When you consistently provide value, people will see you as the authority. They'll trust you, follow you, and eventually, line up to work with you.

Imagine a world with so many potential clients, you can choose who you work with. A world where stress melts away, and your job becomes a daily pleasure. That's the power of content marketing and personal branding!

So, what are you waiting for? Grab that phone, fire up that AI, and start creating! The world is waiting to hear from you. And who knows? Maybe you'll give this presentation next year, sharing your success story with thousands of eager listeners.

Remember again: *"If they can see you—they can trust you."* So, get out there and show them who you are! Your future self will thank you.

AI: The Superpower for Modern Financial Advisors

Imagine for a moment that you're in a race. You're pedalling furiously on your trusty bicycle, giving it your all. Suddenly, a sleek motorcycle zooms past you, leaving you in the dust. That's the difference between working without AI and embracing it in your financial advisory practice. AI isn't just a tool; it's a game-changer—a superpower waiting to be harnessed.

You've probably heard this before, but it bears repeating: AI won't replace financial advisors, but advisors who use AI will replace those who don't. It's not just about staying relevant; it's about soaring to new heights in your profession.

Beyond ChatGPT: A Universe of AI Tools

While ChatGPT has become the poster child for AI, it's just the tip of the iceberg. Let's take a whirlwind tour of the AI landscape:

- **Gemini from Google**: The new kid on the block, trained on Google's vast data resources.
- **Claude from Anthropic**: Known for its nuanced understanding and ethical approach.
- **Copilot from Microsoft**: Your AI sidekick for all things Office and beyond.
- **Perplexity**: Consider it research on steroids, perfect for diving deep into complex topics.
- **You.com**: A search engine with AI superpowers.
- **EasyPeasy AI**: For when you want to create your own AI chatbot without breaking a sweat.
- **Deepseek R1**: The rising AI designed for high-quality reasoning and deep analytical tasks.
- **Qwen from Alibaba**: China's answer to generative AI, bringing a unique take on enterprise and consumer AI.
- **Grok from X**: Elon Musk's AI creation, known for its edgy, witty personality and access to real-time data from X (formerly Twitter).

And that's just scratching the surface! The AI toolbox is expanding faster than you can say *"compound interest"*.

Speaking AI's Language: The Art of Prompting

To truly harness AI's power, you need to learn its language. Enter the world of *"prompts"*—your way of communicating with AI. It's like learning to cast spells, but instead of *"Wingardium Leviosa",* you're using the RISEN framework:

1. **Role**: Who's the AI playing? An advisor? A researcher?
2. **Input**: What information are you feeding it?
3. **Steps**: What's the recipe for success?
4. **Expectation**: What's the end goal?
5. **Narrowing**: Any specific focus or limitations?

Master this, and you'll be crafting AI responses like a virtuoso. And remember, if at first you don't succeed, refine and try again. AI is like a genie—powerful, but it needs the correct instructions to grant your wishes.

Your AI Army: Custom GPTs and Chatbots

Imagine having a team of specialised AI assistants at your beck and call. With custom GPTs, you can create AI experts on any topic. Need a copywriting guru? Create a Copy Master GPT. Want a legal advisor? Craft a Legal Pro GPT. The possibilities are endless.

But why stop there? With tools like EasyPeasy AI, you can create chatbots that serve your clients 24/7. It's like cloning yourself but without the ethical dilemmas. These chatbots can handle inquiries, provide essential advice, and even prospect for you while you sleep. Talk about work-life balance!

AI in Action: Transforming your Practice

Let's get practical. Here's how AI can revolutionise every aspect of your advisory practice:

1. **Know your audience**: Use AI to conduct deep dives into target markets, gaining a deeper understanding of pain points and desires.
2. **Content creation**: Generate blog posts, social media content, and even video scripts in minutes, not hours.
3. **Portfolio analysis**: Upload Excel files and get insights that would take days to compile manually.
4. **Policy comparison**: Let AI sift through the fine print and highlight key policy differences.
5. **Client meetings**: Use tools like Read.ai or Otter.ai to transcribe meetings, generate summaries, and suggest follow-up steps.
6. **Presentations**: Create stunning PowerPoint presentations with Beautiful.ai in seconds.
7. **Research**: Use Chrome extensions like Sider and GPTNote to instantly summarise YouTube videos or lengthy articles.

The AI-Powered Client Experience

Here's a wake-up call: your clients are already using AI. They're coming to meetings more informed and with higher expectations. But don't panic—this is an opportunity to elevate your game. Use AI to stay ahead, providing insights and analysis beyond what your clients can find independently.

The New World of Super-powered Advisors

We've entered a new era in which financial advisors can have super-powers. AI isn't just about doing things faster; it's about doing things you never thought possible. It's about being more productive and efficient and having the time to focus on what really matters—building relationships and providing value to your clients.

Please Don't Miss This Train

The AI revolution isn't coming—it's here. And it's moving at the speed of that motorcycle we discussed earlier. You have a choice: stay on your bicycle and watch the world zoom by or hop on the AI express and lead the pack.

Remember, great power comes with great responsibility (and a lot of fun). So, embrace AI, experiment with it, and let it amplify your human skills. The future of financial advising is here, powered by AI. Are you ready to become a super-advisor?

The Digital Magician's Toolkit: Transforming Insurance Presentations with VR & AR

Welcome to the future of insurance, where reality is optional, but success isn't! Fasten your seatbelts (or should I say, adjust your headsets?) as we dive into the wild world of virtual and augmented reality—where policies float in mid-air, and you can close deals on a virtual beach (sunscreen not included).

VR Meetings: The New Frontier

Imagine hosting client meetings in stunning VR environments. It's like Zoom on steroids! You feel like you are in the same room with the other person. With VR, you can create immersive experiences that leave lasting impressions out of this world!

3D Presentations: Pitch Perfect

One game-changing idea is to create mind-blowing 3D pitches of your practice or strategies. Developing a 3–5-minute pre-recorded presentation in a 3D virtual world using software like Engage is relatively easy. Then, hand your client a VR headset before your meeting starts. They'll be wowed by your tech-savvy approach and captivated by your message. It's like PowerPoint on steroids and a great storytelling tool—minus the boring transitions!

Prospecting in the Metaverse

Don't limit yourself to the real world! Prospect by mingling in VR social spaces like Horizon Worlds from Meta or while playing VR games. Who knew virtual golf could be both fun and productive? Join VR user groups on social media to connect with tech-savvy prospects already embracing this technology. The new generations are more in VR worlds than social media nowadays!

AI-powered Avatars: Your Digital Mini Me

Imagine having your digital clone, powered by artificial intelligence, ready to answer client queries 24/7. These AI avatars can be trained to handle prospects and clients in VR, conduct role-plays, or provide initial consultations. It's like having a tireless assistant, minus the coffee runs and lunch breaks.

The Apple Vision Pro Revolution

With the release of Apple's Vision Pro headset, AR and VR capabilities are becoming more accessible than ever. While the headset is currently on the pricier side, more affordable options like the Meta Quest 3 offer similar features.

As AR technology advances, advisors may soon appear as holograms in clients' homes, blurring the lines between in-person and digital appointments.

Panos already uses VR and AR technology to exercise, meditate, play simulation games, and virtually travel the world. The possibilities are endless!

Getting Started: Baby Steps into the Virtual World

Don't panic if this sounds like sci-fi mumbo-jumbo. You don't need to be Tony Stark to use these tools. Start small:

1. **Invest in a basic VR headset** for your office (Meta Quest 3 is a great, affordable option).
2. **Experiment with simple AR apps** on your smartphone to get a feel for the technology.
3. **Create an introductory VR presentation** to showcase your services.

Remember, being an early adopter doesn't mean you need to be a tech wizard. It's about being open to new possibilities and showing clients you're forward-thinking.

The future of insurance is virtual, it's augmented, and it's knocking on your door. Will you answer? (Make sure you wear trousers if it's a video call!)

By embracing these technologies, you'll impress clients, streamline your processes, and open new avenues for prospecting. So, are you ready to become a digital magician in the insurance world? The virtual stage is set, and the audience is waiting. It's time to put on a show they'll never forget!

Some Last Thoughts and the Mindset of the Phygital Advisor

My dear brothers and sisters in this noble profession, we stand at the precipice of a new era! The digital revolution is not just knocking at our door—it's bursting through, offering us incredible opportunities to transform our profession and our personal lives.

With AI evolution, my friends, we have entered a new world. We now have the potential for superhuman powers at our fingertips! But remember, with great power comes great responsibility. We must learn new skills, adapt, and fly!

It's no longer optional—it's mandatory. We must embrace the kaizen methodology—becoming a little better every day. Start slowly but start! Allocate 5% of your time to experiment and evolve your digital skills. Hire an assistant if you need to—you provide the strategy; they implement it.

Some say, *"Adapt or die,"* but I say, *"Adapt and fly!"* Because even if you don't "die" by not adapting, you're losing a colossal opportunity cost. We need to be the pioneers, the innovators! We must prove our profession is not old-fashioned, technologically backward, or without added value. No! We are one of the most important professions in this world!

Panos Leledakis

Now, we have the tools to educate consumers and change the image of our profession. Let's use this incredible power! Attend seminars, sit again in school, and learn these new skills. It's in our DNA to protect society, and now we have nuclear weapons to do just that!

In this New Digital World, Differentiation is Key

And what is the beautiful thing about these new technologies? They're easier to use than ever before! I challenge you to become phygital advisors—physical and digital! Don't forget what's already working—add technology to the mix.

We need to elevate our skills that technology cannot replicate. Embrace technology, then go beyond it. Empathy, relationships, integrity, consumer education, and the love with which we approach clients to handle misconceptions about our profession—cannot be replicated by AI.

The Result? More Time and More Power

Use that time to break records or create a more balanced life—whatever you desire!

Remember, we now have a tremendous voice. We can easily present ourselves to the world, educate consumers, and make them understand the incredible importance of risk management and financial planning. Insurance is the cleverest financial tool for protection that humanity has ever invented!

Let's Adapt and Fly!

My fellow advisors, let's rise to this challenge! Let's prove that we are not just adapters but innovators, not just survivors but thrivers, the guardians of financial security, the architects of peace of mind, and the champions of protection!

So, I ask you—are you ready to embrace this digital revolution? Are you prepared to become the superhuman advisors of tomorrow? Are you willing to adapt and fly?

Because I tell you this—the future is not something that happens to us. It's something we create. And together, we will create a future where our profession shines brighter than ever before!

Let's adapt and fly, my friends! The sky's not the limit—it's just the beginning!

If you would like to know more about the equipment and AI apps that I use, please feel free to scan this QR code.

Chapter 17
Pivot or Perish
Gail Singh

Gail Singh CIAM, FCCA, ASQ CMQ/OE, PMP, FSCP, is a financial strategist and certified chartered accountant with over 30 years of experience. She has led quality audits, facilitated ISO certifications, and implemented integrated systems in various industries.

As CFO at TOSL Engineering, Gail restructured operations and spearheaded SAP Business One implementation. Since 2010, she has focused on financial advisory, creating tailored solutions for retirement, education, and wealth planning.

A Fellow of the ACCA, and an advocate for poverty eradication, Gail supports the MDRT Foundation and serves as CEO of GMS Associates International Limited, empowering future generations.

Introduction

Along the journey towards success, challenges are a constant. The awareness of the presence of subconsciousness and consciousness within our minds, has a major impact on how we navigate through the "interference" that prevents us from achieving our goals. Our mindsets must be aligned to pivot into action, as and when needed. Failing to embrace challenges and shift gears into resilient action results in delays or not achieving what we set out to do. When this occurs frequently, we are not able to stay relevant and, eventually, we perish.

We can achieve our goals when we, *"learn subconsciously to be successful,"* in the words of Sandro Forte. In his video *Mindset*, Sandro explains that: *"there are gaps between today's intentions and tomorrow's outcomes."* It's called life. Subconsciously, we should remind ourselves of how we feel when we achieve goals. Write down 20 to 30 goals, as though you have already achieved them, and then read them aloud daily at the same time. Recall your last success story and relive that feeling in the quiet of your thoughts. Gradually, you will attract what you want, including the people you need, in order to make it happen.

Consciously, you should remind yourself of why you have the goal and what you must do to remain on course to achieving it.

Adopting the characteristics required for resilience, keeping an attitude of positivity, and taking action to achieve the goal, no matter its size or how you feel, will take you closer to success and inevitable growth and productivity.

Gail Singh

Procrastination vs Prioritisation: A Battle for Productivity

Procrastination and prioritisation are two sides of the same coin, representing vastly different approaches to managing time and tasks. Procrastination, often seen as the enemy of productivity, involves delaying tasks unnecessarily. On the other hand, prioritisation is the act of organising tasks based on their importance and urgency, leading to efficient time management and productivity.

Procrastination stems from various factors, including fear of failure, lack of motivation, and perfectionism. It often results in a cycle of delay, stress, and subpar performance. Individuals caught in this cycle may find themselves overwhelmed by the sheer volume of tasks left undone, creating a sense of executive paralysis.

Prioritisation, however, offers a structured approach to managing tasks. By identifying what is urgent and important, individuals can allocate their time and resources effectively, leading to a sense of accomplishment and reduced stress. Prioritisation requires a clear understanding of one's goals and the discipline to focus on high-impact activities.

Competence, Commitment, Consistency, Care, and Concern: The Five Pillars of Effective Action

1. **Competence**: Competence is having the knowledge and skills that breathe confidence into completing tasks, reaching goals, or performing beyond expectations. It is imperative to remain relevant with continuous learning and development in our core functions and business operations. This creates a competitive edge, ensuring optimal growth.
2. **Commitment**: Commitment is the foundation of any successful endeavour. It involves dedicating oneself to a task

212

or goal, regardless of the challenges that may arise. A committed individual is more likely to persevere through difficulties, maintaining focus and effort until the desired outcome is achieved. Commitment fosters a sense of purpose and direction, essential for overcoming procrastination and ensuring sustained progress.

3. **Consistency**: Consistency is crucial in transforming intentions into results. It involves maintaining regular and sustained efforts towards a goal. Consistent action builds momentum and reinforces positive habits. For instance, consistently prioritising tasks based on their importance can gradually reduce the tendency to procrastinate. Consistency also enhances reliability and trustworthiness, essential traits in both personal and professional settings.

4. **Care**: Care represents the attention and diligence applied to tasks. It involves a genuine concern for the quality and impact of one's work. When individuals care about what they do, they are more likely to invest the necessary time and effort to achieve excellence. This attitude counteracts procrastination by instilling a sense of responsibility and pride in one's work.

5. **Concern**: Concern involves empathy and consideration for the broader implications of one's actions. It encompasses a sense of responsibility towards others and the environment. Individuals who are concerned about the impact of their work are more likely to prioritise tasks that contribute positively to their goals and the well-being of others. This perspective helps in making informed decisions about task prioritisation, and fosters a proactive approach to addressing challenges.

The Cost of Doing Nothing and the Positive Outcomes of Taking Action

The cost of doing nothing can be substantial, both personally and professionally. Procrastination leads to missed opportunities, increased stress, and potential damage to one's reputation. In a professional context, failing to take action can result in lost business, diminished career prospects, and strained relationships with colleagues and clients.

On a personal level, procrastination can lead to a decline in mental and physical health. The constant stress of uncompleted tasks can contribute to anxiety, depression, and other health issues. Additionally, procrastination can strain personal relationships, as unmet obligations and unfulfilled promises erode trust and reliability.

Conversely, taking action yields numerous positive outcomes. Proactive behaviour leads to the timely completion of tasks, reduced stress, and a sense of accomplishment. In a professional setting, taking action enhances productivity, fosters innovation, and builds a reputation for reliability and competence.

Personal growth is another significant benefit of taking action. By consistently addressing tasks and challenges, individuals develop resilience, problem-solving skills, and a sense of self-efficacy. This growth extends to improved mental and physical health, as proactive behaviour reduces stress and promotes a balanced lifestyle.

Resilience in Action: Overcoming Challenges with Determination

Resilience is the ability to bounce back from adversity and maintain focus and determination in the face of challenges. It is a critical attribute for overcoming procrastination and achieving success through prioritisation and proactive behaviour. According to Wilbur Cross in his book *Choices with Clout*,

> *"Resilience is one of the most enviable qualities in people who are healthy in mind, body and spirit, and is a vital factor in achieving goals."*

Resilient individuals possess several key traits:

1. **Optimism**: Resilient individuals maintain a positive outlook, even in difficult situations. They view challenges as opportunities for growth and learning, rather than insurmountable obstacles. This optimism fuels their determination to take action and persevere.
2. **Adaptability**: Resilience involves the ability to adapt to changing circumstances and find new solutions to problems. Adaptable individuals are more likely to adjust their priorities and strategies in response to unforeseen challenges, ensuring continued progress towards their goals.
3. **Self-discipline**: Self-discipline is essential for maintaining consistency and focus. Resilient individuals exercise self-control to avoid distractions and stay committed to their priorities. This discipline helps them overcome the temptation to procrastinate and ensures steady progress.
4. **Support network**: A strong support network provides emotional and practical assistance during challenging times. Resilient individuals cultivate relationships with friends, family, and colleagues who offer encouragement, advice, and resources. This support helps them stay motivated and focused on their goals.
5. **Problem-solving skills**: Effective problem-solving skills enable resilient individuals to identify and address obstacles

efficiently. They approach challenges methodically, breaking them down into manageable parts and developing actionable solutions. This proactive approach reduces the likelihood of procrastination and ensures continuous progress and improvement.

Integrating the Concepts: A Pathway to Success

To achieve success, individuals must integrate the principles of prioritisation, commitment, consistency, care, concern, and resilience into their daily lives. This integration involves adopting a proactive mindset, setting clear goals, and developing effective strategies for task management.

1. **Setting clear goals**: Clear goals provide direction and motivation. By defining specific, measurable, achievable, relevant, and time-bound (SMART) goals, individuals can focus their efforts and track their progress. Clear goals also make it easier to prioritise tasks based on their importance and urgency.
2. **Creating a structured plan**: A structured plan outlines the steps needed to achieve one's goals. This plan should include a prioritised list of tasks, deadlines, and resources. By following a structured plan, individuals can allocate their time and energy effectively, reducing the likelihood of procrastination.
3. **Maintaining a positive mindset**: A positive mindset is essential for overcoming challenges and maintaining motivation. Individuals should practice self-compassion, celebrate their achievements, and view setbacks as opportunities for growth. This mindset fosters resilience and encourages proactive behaviour.

4. **Developing healthy habits**: Healthy habits, such as regular exercise, adequate sleep, and balanced nutrition, contribute to overall well-being and productivity. By prioritising self-care, individuals can maintain the physical and mental energy needed to tackle tasks and achieve their goals.

5. **Seeking support**: Building a strong support network provides valuable resources and encouragement. Individuals should seek feedback, advice, and assistance from trusted friends, family, and colleagues. This support helps them stay motivated and focused on their priorities.

6. **Continuously evaluating and adjusting**: Regular evaluation of one's progress and strategies ensures continued alignment with goals. Individuals should reflect on their achievements, identify areas for improvement, and adjust their plans as needed. This continuous evaluation promotes adaptability and resilience, and is referred to as the DOME Model—Diagnosis, Objectives, Methods, and Evaluation. Diagnosis involves critically reviewing where you are by analysing data and causes for variance of activity and performance for a period, e.g., one month, one quarter, or one year. You then assess your objectives to determine if they were met or not. Questions arise here, e.g., Do you need to adjust for the next period under review based on the results achieved? Was the goal too high or too low? A close review of the methods used in achieving the results for that period then reveals which method produced higher productivity levels and synergy, giving you an understanding of what adjustments are needed, which methods should be discontinued, and which methods should be implemented more. The evaluation is then completed, having investigated gaps in performance and achievement of goals as you enter the next review period. DOME may be implemented for every goal, whether personal or professional. It keeps you

accountable to yourself for your performance, and constantly keeps your "eyes on the ball".

Practical Strategies for Implementation

1. **Time blocking**: Time blocking involves allocating specific blocks of time for different tasks and activities. This technique helps individuals manage their time effectively, reduce distractions, and maintain focus on high-priority tasks. By dedicating time blocks to important activities, individuals can ensure steady progress towards their goals.

2. **The Eisenhower Matrix**: The Eisenhower Matrix is a prioritisation tool that categorises tasks based on their urgency and importance. By dividing tasks into four quadrants (urgent and important, important but not urgent, urgent but not important, and neither urgent nor important), individuals can make informed decisions about where to focus their efforts. This tool helps reduce procrastination and enhances productivity.

3. **The Pomodoro Technique**: The Pomodoro Technique involves working in focused intervals (typically 25 minutes) followed by short breaks. This technique helps individuals maintain concentration, manage their energy levels, and prevent burnout. By breaking tasks into manageable intervals, The Pomodoro Technique reduces the overwhelm associated with large projects, and encourages consistent progress.

4. **Goal-setting frameworks**: Goal-setting frameworks, such as SMART goals, OKRs (objectives and key results), and the GROW model (goal, reality, options, and will), provide structured approaches to defining and achieving goals. These frameworks help individuals clarify their objectives, develop

actionable plans, and track their progress. By setting and pursuing well-defined goals, individuals can enhance their focus, motivation, and resilience.

5. **Mindfulness and stress management**: Mindfulness practices, such as meditation, deep breathing, and journaling, help individuals manage stress and maintain a positive mindset. By incorporating mindfulness into their daily routine, individuals can enhance their self-awareness, reduce anxiety, and improve their ability to stay present and focused. Effective stress management promotes resilience and supports proactive behaviour.

A Goal is Simply a Dream with a Deadline: Harnessing the Law of Attraction

Setting goals is an essential aspect of personal and professional growth. A goal is simply a dream with a deadline—a vision of what one desires to achieve, paired with a commitment to a timeline. This concept transforms abstract dreams into tangible, actionable objectives. When combined with the law of attraction—a philosophy suggesting that positive thoughts bring positive results—goal-setting becomes a powerful tool for success.

Goals provide direction and purpose. They act as a roadmap, guiding individuals towards their desired outcomes. By setting specific, measurable, achievable, relevant, and time-bound (SMART) goals, one can break down a lofty dream into manageable steps. This process not only makes the dream more attainable but also instils a sense of urgency and accountability. A deadline transforms a vague aspiration into a concrete target, fostering motivation and focus.

To achieve a goal, it's crucial to immerse oneself fully in the vision of success. This immersion can be encapsulated by the mantra *"eat, sleep, breathe your goals.*" By making goals an integral part of daily life, individuals reinforce their commitment and maintain consistent focus:

- **Eat**: Every action, even mundane daily activities, can be aligned with one's goals. This means integrating goal-oriented habits into everyday routines, such as reading industry-related materials during meals or discussing progress with peers over coffee.
- **Sleep**: Before bed, visualising the attainment of one's goals can significantly impact the subconscious mind. This practice, often referred to as visualisation, involves imagining the steps to success and the emotions tied to achieving the goal. It prepares the mind to work towards the goal, even during rest.
- **Breathe**: Continually thinking about and reflecting on one's goals keeps them at the forefront of the mind. Deep, mindful breathing exercises while focusing on goals can reduce stress and increase mental clarity, aiding in better decision-making and perseverance.

The law of attraction emphasizes the importance of visual reminders in manifesting dreams. Surrounding oneself with visual cues of goals can reinforce commitment and maintain motivation. Here are a few practical ways to implement this:

1. **Vision boards**: Create a vision board filled with images, quotes, and symbols that represent your goals. Place it in a prominent location where you will see it daily. This constant exposure helps keep your goals top of mind.
2. **Post-it notes**: Use Post-it notes to jot down specific goals or motivational affirmations. Stick them on your mirror, computer, or workspace. These reminders serve as daily affirmations of what you are working towards.

3. **Digital reminders**: Set reminders on your phone or computer that prompt you to take action towards your goals. Digital backgrounds featuring inspirational quotes or images of your goals can also keep you focused.
4. **Branded items**: Use branded items that speak to your goals, such as Million Dollar Round Table (MDRT) branded cups, mugs, bags, pens, and laptop cases.

The Law of Attraction: Think Positive, Act Positive

The law of attraction posits that positive thinking attracts positive outcomes. By maintaining a positive mindset and visualising success, individuals can influence their reality. This doesn't mean that merely thinking about success will bring it about. Instead, it's about fostering a mindset that encourages proactive behaviour, resilience, and an openness to opportunities.

A goal is indeed a dream with a deadline, and by immersing oneself in this vision, using tools like vision boards and the power of positive thinking, success becomes more attainable. The principles of eating, sleeping, and breathing one's goals, combined with the law of attraction, create a powerful synergy that propels individuals towards their aspirations. By surrounding oneself with constant reminders and maintaining a positive outlook, dreams can be transformed into reality.

These strategies enable a better probability of success in achieving goals. Constant subconscious and conscious awareness transforms challenges into opportunities for learning and development. We pivot in the face of adversity and so we do not perish.

Chapter 18
Leveraging Innovation Towards Exceptional Client Service

Sepalika Panagoda

Sepalika Panagoda is a motivator dedicated to helping people achieve their full potential while living the MDRT Whole Person's Life. A Master Financial Advisor® and MDRT Life Member with 18 years of experience, she has earned 11 COT and 4 TOT honours.

Since 2014, Sepalika has led Financial Advisors Incorporation, a leading corporate assurance agency, serving over 12,000 clients globally. As MDRT Country Chair for Sri Lanka, she founded MDRT Sri Lanka, uniting industry leaders and raising membership to over 1,000. She has also contributed to MDRT global events as director, assistant director and speaker.

A passionate volunteer, Sepalika has held leadership roles in Rotary, including assistant governor, past president and international services director for the Rotary Club of Kandy. She is a major donor to the Rotary Foundation.

Sepalika holds a postgraduate diploma in business management from the University of Colombo and is qualified as a Master Financial Advisor® from LIMRA USA. She is married to Air Vice Marshal (Ret.) Dr Asoka Madduma Bandara Amunugama and they have two sons who have excelled in the aviation and marketing industries.

I Want to be Happy

Happiness is the greatest wealth on earth. I want to be happy in all that I do every day and every moment. When I am happy, when I live a fulfilling life, I can give the best back to my world. I feel I am a gift to my world. As a practising whole person, I have nothing to achieve but happiness.

In my daily activity, I ensure that:

1. My family is happy.
2. I am engaged in physical activity.
3. My financial future is secure, and I live within my means.
4. I learn something new.
5. I sustain and grow my leading corporate business.
6. I indulge in a spiritual mindset.
7. I contribute to charity through Rotary and the MDRT Foundation.

I try to inculcate the whole person mindset into my team, daily. Our team is highly energised and motivated.

We embrace ordinary clients and give them an extraordinary experience by helping them achieve future financial security and enabling them to do more with their lives. We team up and invite clients spread all over the world to visit our office, and make them feel at home with a warm Sri Lankan greeting of *"Ayubowan"* at the entrance. They feel at ease and, within no time, start sharing their challenges, sometimes even arriving at solutions themselves. By then, the needs analysis is done, and the right solution is proposed.

Within a few minutes, we complete their documentation electronically and send it for processing, giving 100% focused attention to the client. We celebrate together, exchange gifts, and take photographs like a family.

I make it a point to advise the client, lifting them to the next level, and they leave my office with a very happy mindset. Once a happy client, always a happy client. This is how we have served our clients for 20 years.

We serve more than 10,000 clients across more than 200 companies. My persistency is 100%, and my growth exceeds 20%. Gross domestic happiness in my company is 100%. We celebrate each client interaction —policy reviews, enhancements, new policies, delivering claim cheques, or handing over maturity cheques—as an opportunity to cele-brate. Each phone call, visit, presentation, email, or WhatsApp message is a celebration and an excellent opportunity to be happy and make progress in the business.

We, as a team, apply the same formula to our support staff, couriers, messengers, and virtual staff. They are treated and cared for as unique individuals, and we uplift them every day with our loving kindness. A happy group of external and internal support staff and suppliers complements our clients' happiness.

I ensure that my team is:

1. Inspiring
2. In the right mindset
3. Knowledgeable
4. Skilled

This enables them to perform their duties and extend beyond what is expected of them, for example, growing flowers and plants in the office garden, creating a beautiful path for clients to walk along.

My company, Financial Advisors Incorporation, explores all possible ways to make our clients happy, and that is the formula for business progression.

Fountain of Referrals

My mother and father were government servants who are now retired and earning pensions. They lived a beautiful life, helping villagers, supporting people to build homes, and living independently and happily. They enriched us to grow into a beautiful future.

I witnessed their open-door policy throughout my childhood. The garden gates were always open, and villagers would walk into our home whenever they faced difficulties. Though they arrived with tears, after sharing a meal and having a heartfelt discussion with my parents, they would leave with smiles on their faces.

This holistic and happy lifestyle was deeply rooted in their financial soundness as pensioners. Their rich mindset helped them help others.

This was one of my life dreams—to provide this comfort to every individual I meet.

Sepalika Panagoda

I saw an advertisement in the newspaper for a corporate sales manager to advocate to companies about the importance of group life insurance schemes and group retirement schemes. I knew I could fulfil my life dream by applying for this post at Ceylinco Life, the leading life insurance company in Sri Lanka. I joined them in 2004.

Since then, I have advocated, advised, encouraged, and promoted group retirement schemes and group life insurance schemes for many corporate companies and individual clients in the country. These companies have embraced my teachings and have enriched their staff members by providing life assurance, critical illness policies, education plans, disability cover, and retirement plans.

Any member in a corporate company or organisation can obtain complete life assurance packages at a very nominal group rate. For example, a 35-year-old can obtain Rs 1,000,000 cover for just Rs 2,000 per annum. This is a great attraction for Sri Lanka's poorer communities. My clients, i.e., the staff of these companies and members of organisations, come from diverse livelihoods—couriers, teachers, nurses, doctors, CEOs, garbage collectors, military officers, corporals, sergeants, and general managers. They enjoy the comfort of complete life assurance cover at attractive group rates.

This diverse clientele is a fountain of referrals. I have never needed to advertise myself on social media or forums. Many Sri Lankan communities know that seeking my services guarantees the best comfort, peace of mind, and a path to the next level in life.

When I add one company to my prospect list, it opens up a fountain of referrals, often exceeding 500 prospects. I now have more than 10,000 referrals in my office, and we constantly work on progressing to the next level in our business.

Group financial advisory is a source of immense happiness, a service to all communities, and a fountain of referrals. It allows the business to grow, generates high income, and provides a valuable knowledge base by interacting with an array of inspiring people, including CEOs, chairmen, general managers, and more.

Choosing to be a financial advisor for a corporate clientele has been both a life solution and a path to professional recognition, embracing a never-ending fountain of referrals.

Motherly Love

I believe that my family, friends, clients, and communities see me as a mother, sister, and true friend, who inspires them and lifts them to the next level.

I will continue to strive in this business and give back to the world what it has given me, ensuring I remain worthy of supporting needy communities to thrive.

I am always ready to enrich, motivate, and inspire everyone I meet throughout the day. I feel my clients are fortunate to have me as their advisor because I ensure financial security, peace, and happiness for them and their families. I want my clients to be shining stars. This is the lifestyle I enjoy.

I am devoted to offering special gifts to my clients through what I do. From morning to evening, the people I meet are all progressing in life.

My team members, often perceived as youngsters, are more popular among clients. They enjoy spreading loving kindness to all clients, big or small. We protect and care for them all.

Sri Lanka is a country where all religions coexist harmoniously, and Buddhist philosophy is widely understood. Our team lives by this harmony, and our corporate clients are drawn to the peace of mind this brings. Over the last 20 years, our branch has had zero complaints.

When we feel negativity creeping in, such as anger, jealousy, or hatred, we help each other overcome it and get back on track. My company is a family practising the law of nature.

Each day, my team and I dedicate our time and energy to:

1. Continuous interaction
2. Continuous monitoring and taking corrective action
3. Continuous appreciation
4. Continuous knowledge sharing and learning from one another
5. Enriching the right mindset, knowledge, and skills
6. Learning from mistakes and ensuring they are never repeated
7. Teaching team members how to stand tall in any client communication
8. Focusing on giving million-dollar advice to clients
9. Staying connected with global membership and progressing in life

We ensure that each team member possesses outstanding communication skills.

We are excellent communicators with attractive voices, laughter, smiles, and genuine sincerity. When we give professional advice, we use simple, clear, and precise language that clients easily understand. We translate insurance jargon into household words. We emphasise what we can do rather than dwelling on limitations, turning negative clauses in contracts into positive notes.

Our team members also excel in listening skills. We believe the customer is always right, as only they know what they need and want.

We listen to clients attentively, much like how a mother listens to her child, noticing their body language and helping them feel confident, positive, and comfortable.

For us, a warm Sri Lankan cup of tea often sets the tone for a meaningful conversation. We think with our clients, share their concerns, and see the bigger picture together. Good listening enables us to gather complete facts and propose the right solutions.

We give realistic promises.

We ensure prompt delivery and avoid exaggeration. Clients trust us because our sales presentations are practical and relevant to real-life situations. We are natural, straightforward, and trustworthy. Delivering on our promises builds a beautiful experience for us and our clients daily.

We empathise with clients.

We share their burdens and offer tailored solutions based on their needs. Our clients often view us as best friends, confidantes, and partners in their journeys. Many even say that our names are household names in their families.

We build relationships.

We form lasting personal and professional connections by being accessible every day. Even after benefit cheques are paid, we continue supporting clients, ensuring the next generation is well cared for. Sharing moments with widows and celebrating their resilience is especially rewarding.

We excel at multitasking.

Our team manages multiple tasks simultaneously—sales presentations, premium collections, and policy servicing—thanks to our sophisticated client management systems. Daily planning and activity reviews, conducted virtually or in person, ensure everyone knows what's happening in the business the next day.

We treat clients like family.

Embrace Victory

A winning mindset is a way of life for me and my team members. Any client who rarely says no to our solutions has missed an opportunity, but we remain undeterred. We are winners, trendsetters, and progress-makers, helping clients embrace their victories alongside ours.

MDRT has made a remarkable contribution to my journey, shaping my mindset to take the baton forward and thrive.

- MDRT made me feel significant and accepted.
- MDRT introduced me to a global family.
- MDRT united my team members and Sri Lankan members.
- MDRT taught me how to embrace victory and enrich the lives of others.

I walk MDRT, talk MDRT, think MDRT, and live MDRT's Whole Person concept. This philosophy has balanced my mindset and guided me to serve those in need. Winning is now a lifestyle embedded in my mindset.

As the CEO of Financial Advisors Incorporation, Ceylinco Life, I am deeply grateful for the progression I've made. My dream now is to make myself redundant and pass the baton to my capable team members.

My beloved husband, our business consultant, guides and corrects me daily. He is my greatest gift on earth, a treasure trove of wisdom, and a blessing to my clients.

Together, we embrace victory every day.

Part Six

Succession Planning and Futureproofing

Chapter 19
Trace or Fingerprint?
Kyriakos Chatzistefanou

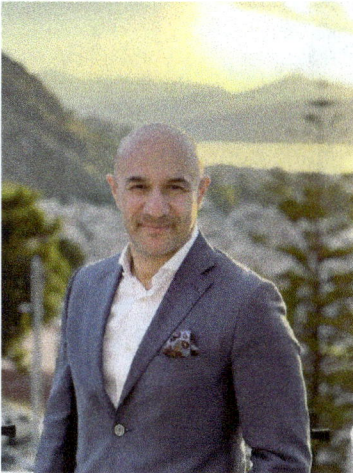

Kyriakos Chatzistefanou began his insurance career in 1992 with Alico (A.I.G. Group), which later became MetLife and is now NN Hellas. With over 30 years of experience, he has been a life member of the Greek Circle of Successful Agents in MetLife and has earned five global distinctions for contract persistence.

He holds a diploma in management from Kingston University (2007) and a diploma from the Chartered Management Institute (2008). As an MDRT Life Member since 2017, Kyriakos has served in leadership roles, including Area Chair, Country Chair, Zone Chair, and Region Chair for MDRT, reflecting his dedication to professional excellence.

Since 1999, Kyriakos has shared his expertise through training seminars and lectures worldwide, specialising in every stage of the insurance sales cycle. As a speaker, he has had the opportunity to present at international events, including MDRT's annual conferences in the USA since 2018.

Kyriakos is the author of three books. *19 Stars Insurance Leaders* (2009) was co-authored with Dimitrios Kastrinakis; *Philotimo* (2020) explores ethical business values; and *Referrals! Is your fingerprint strong enough?* (2022) is published in Greek, English, and Polish, with worldwide distribution. His books are featured in libraries across the world.

Kyriakos is married to Pulcheria, and they have two children, Foteini and Panagiotis. His motto, *"We are only limited in our minds by the boundaries we set,"* reflects his commitment to inspiring others.

Introduction

The goal of this chapter is to inspire, motivate, and direct towards giving, reciprocity, creativity, fair play, and cooperation for the common good of all—a concept that has been notably absent from our daily lives lately.

> *"If the sales process is our identity as insurance agents, sharing our ideas with all our colleagues, without compromise, is our 'fingerprint'. And if we repeat this often, then it boosts our confidence and the character of the professional within us."*

> — Kyriakos Chatzistefanou

In the definition of *'fingerprint'*, "each person's finger has a unique embossed shape on its surface [...] and as it is used to grip things, it leaves unique greasy marks (fingerprints) on the objects it touches."[1] These fingerprints are unique. By linking the above definition to our profession and the insurance consultant, I would say that each of us has our own character and behaviour when it comes to communication. When we communicate with each prospective client and each human being, we leave our own unique impression. So, it is this impression we are talking about, and whether, according to the prospective client's criteria, it will be interpreted as a trace or a fingerprint.

This difference between the trace and the fingerprint will be confirmed and validated by each prospective client through each stage in the sales process. And that's where each one of us will meet our limits—or not. This is the opportunity where, through the sales process, we can touch them.

To know your limits, to reconcile, and why not fall in love with *"reaching your limits"*, just as I have fallen in love with it and become clearly aware of how powerful my decibel is; to be able to reach my limits when I turn up the volume daily, and stay there as long as I can without *"it costing me"* but enjoying it; to live through this profession as if on a journey, and to share it daily with friends, clients, family, and colleagues, just as I do with you after exactly 32 years.

This *"fingerprint"*, *"reaching your limits"*, the *"decibel level"*, and *"volume"*, are our uniqueness and our competitive advantage. It is the combination of the traits of our personality expressed through the projects and services we offer and the results we want to deliver for our clients and ourselves. Our meetings with prospective clients must have one single goal: that prospective clients see this *"fingerprint"* as a sign, an opportunity, and a challenge to work with us.

---

1. https://el.wikipedia.org/wiki/Αποτύπωμα - https://cutt.ly/KX8RkKC - Translation from the Greek Wikipedia – (Retrieved: 20/06/2022)

The volume and the decibel level are not the limits of your professional endurance, where you experience a "danger ahead" signal—a tunnel without light, a flight in the fog. It is those limits that propel you to open your wings and fly to where you have dreamed of through this profession, and have always sought in your life. The volume and the decibel level are the push towards that direction, just as eagles push their chicks from their nest into the void to learn to fly. Every beginning is difficult, and it is true that we don't love change, but they're the only ones that can lead us to new professional success.

A Personal Story

In 2019, I travelled with my mother to New York. It was a leisure trip combined with business commitments. Although I needed to stay focused on my work, I also wanted to give my 73-year-old mother the best experience. It was her first time making a transatlantic trip and only the second time she had ever flown. We stayed at the historic Art Deco Hotel Edison at 47th and Broadway, right in the heart of New York City, just a block away from Times Square.

Throughout the trip, my mother was constantly anxious about the specifics and *difficulties* of the journey, including not knowing the English language at all. Another serious difficulty was her mobility, as she often experienced tiredness in her legs. Despite her objections, I took on the responsibility and pleasure of travelling with her so she could experience the other side of the world and see with her own eyes what *"America"* and *"New York"* meant.

One morning, I woke up at 4:00 am as usual, due to jet lag. I went into my mother's room to check on her, but she wasn't there. I assumed she must have gone to the bathroom. After waiting a while, I knocked on the bathroom door, but she didn't respond. I called her name but still got no answer. Worried, I opened the door and didn't find her inside. As

I searched the apartment again, realising my mother was gone, I quickly dressed and hurried down to the hotel lobby, hoping to find her there or at the hotel entrance.

My mother has been a smoker for years, and despite our disagreements, cigarettes are one of her delights. So, the only logical conclusion at 4:00 am was that she was enjoying a cigarette at the hotel entrance. However, I didn't see her in the lobby or at the hotel entrance. A cold sweat washed over me.

As I stood there, desperate and panicking, I suddenly saw my mother smiling and coming from the back of 47th Street with a coffee in her hand. At the corner of 7th and 47th, there was a coffee shop, but it was closed at that hour since everything opens after 5:00 am. Relieved but upset, I wondered how she had managed to find coffee. It was her need for a morning cigarette that drove her to cross her boundaries, ignoring the dangers and my instructions for a safe stay in New York.

The dialogue that followed was unique:

"Where have you been? I've been looking for you!" "I went to get a coffee." "Didn't we agree to only go out together outside the hotel?" "Yes, but I wanted coffee because I'm up now and I can't sleep. I didn't want to wake you up. I want to enjoy my cigarette with a cup of coffee." "And you set out at 4:00 in the morning to find coffee in New York when everything's closed?" "I asked where there was a coffee shop and they told me on the corner." "And it wasn't closed?" "It was closed, but there were people inside making preparations for the opening." "And how did you arrange to get coffee?" "I knocked on the door. A sweet girl came and opened it, and said something I couldn't understand. I told her 'coffee', showed her the money, and she brought me coffee. It was easy after all," she said and walked off as if nothing had happened.

Kyriakos Chatzistefanou

Despite her limited travel experience, mobility issues, and not knowing a word of English beyond *"coffee"*, my mother pushed her limits. She discovered that there are no boundaries, no matter the difficulties we perceive. This experience taught her—and once again taught me—that sometimes things are easier than we think if we decide to push our limits, to pass our boundaries. Now, she can proudly share her adventure with her friends, and I can share it with you.

A Reflection on our Profession

Dear colleagues, our profession is not just a *job*, it is a *vocation*. We are not just *"an insurance agent"* but rather *"their consultant"*. The result of our work is not *"an insurance policy"* but *"a life and security policy"* and finally, *"a human relationship"*.

Joe Jordan in his book, *"Living a Life of Significance"* claims:

"You have to recognise that you do something very significant—you could be the most important person in someone's life. A family continues, or a business continues, or a legacy is spawned for generations because of your activities. You've got to not only know it, you've got to believe it and feel it." [2]

Today's clients are informed because they have understood the need; because they want to be clients, and because they are ready to buy. So, knowing that this is the case, our only concern should be how exactly the process of collaboration will be initiated in the prospective client's mind when we leave the first appointment and, at the same time, how the process of long-term professional support will stay in ours.

---

2. Joseph W. Jordan, "Living a Life of Significance" (2011), page 66, section: "So get Inspired", paragraph 3

By keeping this human relationship close to you, turn up your volume a little bit more and eventually you will find the correct decibel, the limits of your own endurance. This will always define and align each relationship towards the right direction, lasting in time and being healthy.

The Journey of Relationships

Our relationship with what we represent is a journey over time with a destination. Each relationship we have with a client is a mission. One mission may be small and brief, while another is long and enduring. Together, they are all an addition to the profession of an insurance consultant in all corners of the globe—a *guarantee* for the future of the insurance profession, and the concept of insurance.

How could Edward Lloyd have imagined what the *"insurance map"* would look like today, after his own contribution? How could Alexander the Great have envisioned that his strategic tactics on the battlefield would be taught in the world's greatest universities as modern management tactics? How could Aristotle, Plato, Sophocles, and other ancient philosophers have imagined that their teachings would resonate globally for centuries, influencing people to evolve and strive for the common good?

We are not far from such success ourselves, however romantic, utopian, or impossible it may sound. Life has shown that the *"impossible"* is achievable, that the weak often triumph, and that the youngest can surpass the oldest. Somewhere in between is where you are. So, turn up your volume today, and each day turn it up a bit more, until you reach your perfect decibel.

Our attitude during meetings, our statements, our communication patterns, our style, our storytelling, and our communicativeness should reflect our passion, faith, knowledge, and love for what we represent. These qualities should allow each prospective client to understand our uniqueness, professionalism, and differentiation from others in our field.

The *"fingerprint"* is none other than our core identity and professional existence that is illuminated through our emotions and way of working, and validated through the sales process and all it entails. For those of us who are older, it is our experience that is the most significant guarantee of a successful partnership with prospective clients. For younger colleagues, however, this guarantee is replaced by passion, the "thirst", the subtlety, the promise for the future, and the will to last in this profession. When accompanied by honesty, integrity, diligence, and *"philotimo"* (a Greek concept embodying honour and integrity), this *"fingerprint"* becomes so pure, transparent, and crystal clear that it instils confidence in prospective clients to work with us.

Pushing the Decibel

I remember throughout my professional career often asking myself the same thing: "How many decibels can you handle today, Kyriakos?" And so I went on. In each appointment, I turned up the volume more and more, and still do every day, and what I discovered is not the volume itself but a pervasive harmony that challenges and motivates me each time, for that little bit more.

This is how our presence in meetings must be etched in the memory of prospective clients. When life insurance is discussed, we should be their first choice, their immediate reference, the example, and the differentiator. It is precisely when approaching prospective clients, using the process of "communication-contact-meeting", that we leave our own unique *"insurance fingerprint"*—after we have turned up our volume a bit more and tried once again to reach our limits and listen to the intensity of the decibel.

A *"fingerprint"* represents our lasting impression, formed when our main concern during meetings is the life insurance sales process. It also reflects a non-negotiable principle: the importance of helping others understand their duty to protect their loved ones.

The life insurance sales process has evolved. Client needs have changed, and our skills must adapt accordingly. However, our principles remain an integral part of the cornerstone of our ideals and ethics and are highly valued in our collaboration. Two of these fundamental principles, which I have observed over the years to add distinct value in the eyes of the client, are respect for their experience and respect for the inexperience of our young colleagues, regardless of the companies they work for. This attitude alone adds the value we need in the eyes of our clients.

Be Prepared for Opportunity

Being in front of a client means we've invested time, energy, effort, and money. Standing before a client is our opportunity to be productive and beneficial—for them and for us. It is the moment where we decide whether we want to stand out or not, to truly be useful or not.

I become useful when, after meeting with my client, they begin to care more about their future and feel the need to protect their loved ones. As our colleague Vanessa Bucklin states in her book, *"The Penultimate Step"*:[3]

---

3. Vanessa Bucklin, "The Penultimate Step" (2020), page 113, "Philotimo", paragraph 2-3

"We keep our promises, but more importantly, we help others keep their promises. You buy life insurance because you love someone. This makes my job so rewarding; I just need to go out and find people who love each other. I have the privilege of protecting lives and fulfilling that gesture of love. There isn't a more honourable task."

So that's why I do it. And when you do it for that reason and not solely for the purpose of expanding your portfolio, then your face shines and you realise that you can turn up your volume a little bit more every day. That's when you leave your own fingerprint on your clients or prospective clients.

Lessons from Great Mentors

Our career is like a ship, and its direction depends on how well we steer it. As the Greek saying goes, *"You can tell how good a captain is by how they manage the storm."*

But no captain was good when they left their helm, and no captain was good when they did not pass on their knowledge to the younger ones.

I have been lucky in this 32-year journey, because I've been around people who have truly behaved like good captains, whether they were colleagues, directors, or administrative staff. In those 32 years I have met some of the strongest mentors in our industry—mainly in Greece but also abroad, through MDRT. I received the best of what they were trying to impart to me and what was most feasible for me to implement, according to my own temperament and beliefs. So, I marched with them in my professional journey as if they were an unwritten Code of Success. They have left their *"fingerprints"* on the Greek and worldwide insurance markets, and continue to do so, serving our profession selflessly for the benefit of everyone. It would be difficult to name them all, but they do know this, and that is the greatest value in a relationship. With all of them—those who are in Greece and those abroad —either through the company I work for, my fellow competitors, or through the MDRT association, we are bound by strong friendships based on appreciation, mutual support, and fair play.

So, I was lucky, but I never expected, nor demanded, that fate hand me success without having to work for it. I was prepared, and when opportunities came along, I committed myself fully, in order to get the best possible outcome. And that's what I urge you to do too. Prepare for what you have decided to pursue, properly, with passion and love—to represent the insurance consultancy profession to the best of your ability. Always be prepared, and be there for your clients when you need to be there. If you do this, then you can rest assured that "luck" will do its work well.

Dream Big

Vincent van Gogh once said, *"I dream my painting and I paint my dream."* This sentiment reflects the spirit of great visionaries, from Alexander the Great and the philosophers of Ancient Greece to a multitude of modern innovators, all of whom have left their positive mark on the history of the world.

Edward Lloyd had a similar vision for the insurance profession, and so many people today continue to follow his inspiring vision. I would like to follow the same path as these visionaries, and mentally go along with them—all of us together, without thinking competitively, and making the effort to leave a *"fingerprint"* rather than just a *"trace"*.

As Thomas Edison famously said:

"I have not failed. I've just found 10,000 ways that won't work."

This mindset of resilience and perseverance is essential to achieving our goals.

Conclusion

Dear colleagues and friends, *"We are only limited in our minds by the boundaries we set."* This is my favourite motto, and it has guided my journey.

In closing, I wish for every one of your dreams to come true because they are yours; you deserve them, you created them, and only you can achieve them!

———

Disclaimer: This chapter was created from existing material, mostly motivational ideas and concepts from my book "Referrals! Is Your Fingerprint Strong Enough?", adapted anew, but also with new additions and experiences, for the needs of the publication of this collective book by my colleagues from the International Study Group (ISG), of which I am a member.

Chapter 20
Seamless Succession
Hari Maragos

Hari Maragos is a Certified Financial Planner® professional and SMSF (Self-Managed Superannuation Fund) Specialist Advisor™ with over 30 years of experience in financial services. He runs a boutique, family office style practice in Melbourne, focusing on multi-generational family wealth management.

Hari holds a Master's of Financial Planning (estate planning specialisation), a double degree in accounting and banking & finance, and is currently pursuing a Master's of Law. In addition to his practice, he lectures at universities and TAFE. A passionate mentor, Hari coaches and mentors financial planners worldwide through his 'Advice Coach' brand, and organises global study tours for advisors.

Hari Maragos

Hari is a member of STEP and MDRT, and serves as a Life Happens™ Ambassador for Australasia/Oceania. He has received several accolades, including the FAAA's 'Distinguished Service Award' in 2012.

An advocate for the outdoors, Hari is a nationally accredited 4WD instructor and supports charities like the Future2 Foundation and Four Wheel Drive Victoria. He has authored two books; *25 Reasons why you Should use a Financial Planner,* and *Change for Good – The 5Ws and 1H of Financial Planning.*

Abstract

This chapter offers a structured approach to creating a seamless succession plan for financial advisory practices, utilising the Kaizen methodology and SMART goals. By defining clear succession objectives, analysing the current state of the practice, identifying key stakeholders, locating talent, establishing realistic timelines, and implementing comprehensive training programs, the chapter provides a detailed action plan.

It emphasises the importance of continuous improvement, transparent client communication, and proactive engagement. Readers will learn how to ensure business continuity, maintain client relationships, and achieve a smooth transition of responsibilities. This guide is essential for financial advisors aiming to prepare their practice for a successful future through effective succession planning.

Seamless Succession Planning for Financial Advisory Practices Using Kaizen and SMART Goals

Introduction

Succession planning is a crucial element in ensuring the longevity and continued success of professional financial advisory practices. Implementing a well-structured succession plan can be challenging, but applying the Kaizen approach of continuous improvement, along with the SMART goal framework, offers a clear path to success.

This chapter provides a comprehensive guide to developing a seamless succession plan using the 5W1H method. Through actionable steps, tips, traps to avoid, and insights from notable figures throughout history, readers will learn how to effectively manage and execute a succession strategy.

What: Define Succession Goals

"Setting goals is the first step in turning the invisible into the visible."

— Tony Robbins

"Goals are dreams with deadlines."

— Diana Scharf Hunt

Action plan:

1. **Set clear objectives**
   - Define the primary goals of the succession plan. Key objectives typically include ensuring business continuity, preserving client relationships, and facilitating a smooth transition of responsibilities. Clear objectives provide a solid foundation and direction for the entire succession process.
   - **SMART goal example:** *"Within the next 12 months, create a comprehensive succession plan that ensures a 90% client retention rate during the transition."*
2. **Document the process**
   - Document the succession plan's objectives and share them with key stakeholders. Written goals ensure clarity and provide a reference point throughout the process.
   - **SMART goal example:** *"By the end of Q1, distribute a documented succession plan to all senior team members for feedback."*

Tips:

- **Clarity and detail:** Clearly outline each goal to avoid ambiguity. Specific and detailed goals are more likely to be understood and achieved.
- **Involve stakeholders:** Engage senior staff in defining objectives to ensure alignment and buy-in. Their involvement can provide valuable insights and foster commitment.

Traps to avoid:

- **Vague goals:** Avoid setting unclear or general goals that are difficult to measure or achieve. Specificity is key to effective goal-setting.
- **Ignoring stakeholder input:** Not incorporating feedback from key personnel can lead to misaligned objectives and resistance to the plan.

"Without goals and plans to reach them, you are like a ship that has set sail with no destination."

— Fitzhugh Dodson

Why: Analyse the Current State

"The first step toward change is awareness. The second step is acceptance."

— Nathaniel Branden

"The first step in solving a problem is to recognise that it does exist."

— Zig Ziglar

Action plan:

1. **Conduct a comprehensive assessment**
   - Evaluate the current state of the practice, including key personnel, client portfolios, and potential succession challenges. This assessment should identify strengths, weaknesses, opportunities, and threats (SWOT analysis).
   - **SMART goal example:** *"Within the next 6 months, complete a detailed assessment of the practice, identifying potential successors and areas requiring improvement."*
2. **Identify critical roles and responsibilities**
   - List all critical roles within the practice and the responsibilities associated with each. Understanding these roles is essential for identifying gaps and planning for smooth transitions.
   - **SMART goal example:** *"By the end of the quarter, create a detailed role and responsibility matrix for all key positions."*

Tips:

- **Thorough evaluation:** Conduct in-depth assessments to fully understand the current state. Use various tools like SWOT analyses, employee surveys, and performance reviews.
- **Future-proofing:** Consider future challenges and opportunities in the analysis. Think about profession trends, technological advancements, and evolving client needs.

Traps to avoid:

- **Incomplete data:** Relying on incomplete or outdated information can lead to flawed analysis and ineffective planning.
- **Overlooking soft skills:** Ignoring the importance of interpersonal skills and cultural fit can jeopardise team dynamics and client relationships.

"Understanding the past is key to success in the future."

— Charles Kettering

Who: Identify Key Stakeholders

"Alone we can do so little; together we can do so much."

— Helen Keller

"Teamwork is the ability to work together towards a common vision; the ability to direct individual accomplishments towards organisational objectives. It is the fuel that allows common people to attain uncommon results."

— Andrew Carnegie

Action plan:

1. **List key personnel**
   - Identify current advisors, potential successors, support staff, and other key stakeholders. This includes individuals who will be directly affected by the succession plan, and those who can influence its success.
   - **SMART goal example:** *"Within 2 months, compile a comprehensive list of key stakeholders involved in the succession process."*
2. **Engage and communicate**
   - Ensure regular communication with all identified stakeholders to keep them informed and involved. Effective communication fosters collaboration and reduces resistance.
   - **SMART goal example:** *"Establish a bi-monthly meeting schedule to update all stakeholders on the succession plan's progress."*

Tips:

- **Inclusive approach:** Involve all relevant stakeholders to ensure a broad perspective and gain diverse insights. This can include employees at various levels, clients, and even external advisors.
- **Clear communication channels:** Maintain open and transparent communication. Use various channels such as meetings, emails, and newsletters to keep everyone informed.

Traps to avoid:

- **Exclusion:** Failing to include all relevant stakeholders can lead to resistance and gaps in the plan. Ensure that no key individuals are overlooked.
- **Lack of communication:** Poor communication can result in misunderstandings and lack of buy-in. Regular updates and open dialogue are essential.

"Unity is strength... When there is teamwork and collaboration, wonderful things can be achieved."

— Mattie Stepanek

Where: Locate Talent and Skills

"The only thing worse than training your employees and having them leave is not training them and having them stay."

— Henry Ford

"An organisation's ability to learn, and translate that learning into action, rapidly, is the ultimate competitive advantage."

— Jack Welch

Action plan:

1. **Internal talent review**
   - Assess existing staff to identify potential successors within the organisation. This involves evaluating their skills, performance, and readiness for leadership roles.
   - **SMART goal example:** *"Conduct internal talent assessments and identify at least three potential successors within 3 months."*
2. **External talent search**
   - If necessary, look externally to find qualified candidates. This can provide fresh perspectives and bring in new skills that may not be present internally.
   - **SMART goal example:** *"Initiate an external search for potential successors, aiming to identify at least two qualified candidates within 6 months."*

Tips:

- **Comprehensive evaluation:** Consider both internal and external candidates to find the best fit. Use a combination of performance reviews, 360-degree feedback, and skills assessments.
- **Skills development:** Invest in training programs to develop internal talent. This can include leadership development, technical training, and soft skills enhancement.

Traps to avoid:

- **Narrow focus:** Only considering internal or external candidates can limit options. A balanced approach can provide the best pool of talent.
- **Ignoring development needs:** Failing to invest in potential successors' development can hinder readiness. Ongoing training and development are essential for preparing successors.

"Investing in your team's strengths is the greatest investment you can make."

— Unknown

When: Establish Timelines

"A goal without a timeline is just a dream."

— Robert Herjavec

"The key is not spending time, but investing it."

— Stephen R. Covey

Action plan:

1. **Create a detailed timeline**
   - Develop a timeline for the succession plan, including key

milestones and deadlines. This timeline should be realistic and account for all necessary steps in the process.

- o **SMART goal example:** *"Develop a succession timeline with key milestones to be completed over the next 18 months."*

2. **Set regular checkpoints**
   - o Establish regular checkpoints to review progress and make adjustments, as needed. This helps in keeping the plan on track and addressing any issues promptly.
   - o **SMART goal example:** *"Schedule quarterly review meetings to assess progress and make necessary adjustments."*

Tips:

- **Realistic timelines:** Set achievable deadlines to ensure steady progress. Consider the complexity of the tasks and the availability of resources.
- **Flexibility:** Be prepared to adjust timelines, as needed. Unexpected challenges may arise, and flexibility ensures that the plan remains feasible.

Traps to avoid:

- **Unrealistic deadlines:** Setting impractical deadlines can lead to stress and failure. Ensure that the timelines are reasonable and attainable.
- **Ignoring progress reviews:** Failing to review progress regularly can result in unnoticed issues. Regular checkpoints are essential for monitoring and adjusting the plan.

"Time is the most valuable thing a man can spend."

— Theophrastus

How: Implement Training Programs

"Tell me and I forget, teach me and I may remember, involve me and I learn."

— Benjamin Franklin

"Learning is not attained by chance, it must be sought for with ardour, and attended to with diligence."

— Abigail Adams

Action plan:

1. **Develop training programs**
   - Create comprehensive training programs covering technical skills, client relationship management, and practice-specific knowledge. These programs should be tailored to the needs of the successors and the practice.
   - **SMART goal example:** *"Within 6 months, implement a training program for potential successors, including quarterly evaluations."*
2. **Mentorship and shadowing**
   - Establish mentorship programs where potential successors can learn from current advisors. This hands-on experience is invaluable for transferring knowledge and building confidence.

- ○ **SMART goal example:** *"Pair potential successors with current advisors for a 12-month mentorship program, starting next quarter."*

Tips:

- **Structured training:** Ensure training programs are well-structured and cover all necessary areas. Use a combination of formal training, workshops, and on-the-job learning.
- **Mentorship opportunities:** Provide ample opportunities for hands-on learning and mentorship. This can include shadowing, coaching sessions, and regular feedback.

Traps to avoid:

- **Insufficient training:** Inadequate training can leave successors unprepared. Comprehensive and ongoing training is essential.
- **Lack of mentorship:** Not providing mentorship can hinder knowledge transfer. Mentors play a crucial role in guiding and supporting successors.

"Do not wait to strike till the iron is hot; but make it hot by striking."

— William Butler Yeats

Client Communication Strategy

"The single biggest problem in communication is the illusion that it has taken place."

— George Bernard Shaw

"Communication—the human connection—is the key to personal and career success."

— Paul J. Meyer

Action plan:

1. **Develop a communication plan**
   - Create a detailed communication plan to inform clients about the succession process and address their concerns. Clear and proactive communication helps maintain trust and confidence.
   - **SMART goal example:** *"Develop and roll out a client communication plan within 3 months, ensuring all clients are informed within the next 6 months."*

2. **Client introduction meetings**
   - Arrange meetings between clients and potential successors to build trust and familiarity. These meetings provide an opportunity to address any client concerns directly.
   - **SMART goal example:** *"Schedule introductory meetings between clients and successors within the next 9 months, aiming for 100% client coverage."*

Tips:

- **Transparent communication:** Be open and transparent with clients about the succession plan. This helps in building trust and mitigating any concerns.
- **Proactive engagement:** Actively engage clients to address their concerns and build trust. Regular updates and personal interactions can reassure clients about the continuity of service.

Traps to avoid:

- **Poor communication:** Inadequate communication can lead to client dissatisfaction and loss of business. Ensure that the communication plan is thorough and timely.
- **Ignoring client feedback:** Failing to consider client feedback can result in missed opportunities to improve the transition process. Client feedback is valuable for refining the succession plan.

"Good communication is the bridge between confusion and clarity."

— Nat Turner

Continuous Improvement and Monitoring

"Without continual growth and progress, such words as improvement, achievement, and success have no meaning."

— Benjamin Franklin

"Progress is impossible without change, and those who cannot change their minds cannot change anything."

— George Bernard Shaw

Action plan:

1. **Regular reviews and feedback**
   - Continuously monitor the succession plan's progress and seek feedback from stakeholders. Regular reviews help identify areas for improvement and make necessary adjustments.
   - **SMART goal example:** *"Conduct quarterly reviews of the succession plan's implementation and gather feedback from key stakeholders."*
2. **Adapt and improve**
   - Implement a system for continuous improvement, incorporating feedback and lessons learned. This approach ensures that the succession plan remains relevant and effective.
   - **SMART goal example:** *"Within 12 months, establish a continuous improvement process to adapt and refine the succession plan based on feedback and performance metrics."*

Tips:

- **Continuous monitoring:** Regularly monitor the plan's progress and impact. Use key performance indicators (KPIs) to measure success and identify areas for improvement.

- **Feedback loop:** Create a feedback loop with stakeholders to gather insights and make informed adjustments. This ensures that the plan evolves with the changing needs of the practice.

Traps to avoid:

- **Stagnation:** Allowing the plan to become static can lead to its ineffectiveness. Continuous improvement is essential for maintaining relevance and success.
- **Ignoring feedback:** Overlooking feedback can result in persistent issues and missed opportunities for enhancement. Actively seek and incorporate feedback.

"Continuous improvement is better than delayed perfection."

— Mark Twain

Conclusion

Creating a seamless succession plan for financial advisory practices requires a structured approach, continuous improvement, and precise goal setting. By following the Kaizen principles and utilising the 5W1H framework along with SMART goals, practices can ensure a smooth transition, maintain client relationships, and sustain business continuity.

Implementing the outlined action plan will help readers systematically develop and execute an effective succession strategy, preparing their practice for a successful future. By integrating these timeless insights and practical strategies, financial advisory practices can navigate the complexities of succession planning with confidence and foresight.

This comprehensive approach ensures that the practice survives and thrives through the transition, securing its legacy for future generations.

References

- Adams, A.: "*Learning is not attained by chance, it must be sought for with ardour and attended to with diligence.*"
- Branden, N.: "*The first step towards change is awareness. The second step is acceptance.*"
- Carnegie, A.: "*Teamwork is the ability to work together toward a common vision. The ability to direct individual accomplishments toward organisational objectives. It is the fuel that allows common people to attain uncommon results.*"
- Covey, S. R.: "*The key is not spending time, but investing it.*"
- Ford, H.: "*The only thing worse than training your employees and having them leave is not training them and having them stay.*"
- Franklin, B.: "*Tell me and I forget, teach me and I may remember, involve me and I learn.*"
- Herjavec, R.: "*A goal without a timeline is just a dream.*"
- Hunt, D. S.: "*Goals are dreams with deadlines.*"
- Keller, H.: "*Alone we can do so little; together we can do so much.*"
- Meyer, P. J.: "*Communication—the human connection —is the key to personal and career success.*"
- Robbins, T.: "*Setting goals is the first step in turning the invisible into the visible.*"
- Shaw, G. B.: "*Progress is impossible without change, and those who cannot change their minds cannot change anything.*"

Hari Maragos

- Shaw, G. B.: "*The single biggest problem in communication is the illusion that it has taken place.*"
- Turner, N.: "*Good communication is the bridge between confusion and clarity.*"
- Twain, M.: "*Continuous improvement is better than delayed perfection.*"
- Welch, J.: "*An organisation's ability to learn, and translate that learning into action, rapidly, is the ultimate competitive advantage.*"
- Yeats, W. B.: "*Do not wait to strike till the iron is hot; but make it hot by striking.*"
- Ziglar, Z.: "*The first step in solving a problem is to recognise that it does exist.*"

Chapter 21
Making For a Better Tomorrow
K. Venka

K. Venka is a seasoned financial services director with over 30 years of experience. A graduate of the National University of Singapore with a double major in economics and statistics, Venka began his career in 1992 and has become a respected leader in the profession.

As a quarter-century MDRT Life Member celebrating his 30th qualification year in 2024, Venka has achieved numerous accolades, including the Top 5 Financial Planner Award by the Financial Planning Association of Singapore (FPAS). He founded Vision Financial in 1999, leading a team of over 30 consultants serving clients across Singapore and Asia.

Venka is also a dedicated mentor, having served as MDRT MCC Chairperson for Singapore. A sought-after speaker and fundraiser, Venka shares his expertise regionally and supports various charitable causes. An accomplished author, he wrote *Anchoring Success*, sharing insights from his career to inspire readers towards financial security. His motto, *"A hungry stomach, an empty wallet, and a broken heart teach you the most valuable lessons in life,"* reflects his dedication to helping others succeed.

Venka's legacy is rooted in his commitment to integrity, mentorship, and service, guiding Vision Financial to deliver impactful solutions for clients, locally and globally.

Introduction

In a world driven by the relentless pursuit of success, the financial advisory profession is no exception. The journey towards building a resilient and enduring business is paved with challenges and milestones that test the mettle of financial advisors. To navigate this complex landscape, one must embrace both the immediate joys and the long-term gratifications that come with dedication and perseverance. The concepts of gratification and gratitude are instrumental in this journey, serving as guiding principles that shape our professional lives and foster a fulfilling business environment.

Gratification and Gratitude

Gratification

In the pursuit of resilience in business, the dynamics of gratification and gratitude play a pivotal role. Gratification, often associated with immediate rewards or short-term wins, holds profound significance when viewed through the lens of long-term success. While the allure of quick victories may propel us forward, it is the appreciation of smaller, more frequent joys that sustains us on the journey.

Allow me to illustrate this point with a personal anecdote from my own experience. In the early days of my business venture in the 90s, I had a remarkable partnership with my late business partner. We shared a commitment not only to our shared goals but also to nurturing a supportive and gratifying work environment. This commitment was the cornerstone of our success and growth.

We devised a weekly ritual that became the highlight of our entrepreneurial journey. Every Friday afternoon, like clockwork, we would meet at our favourite ice cream shop. It was our sanctuary, our refuge from the demands of the week. Sitting down at 4 or 5 pm, we would each take turns recounting the business we had conducted from Saturday to Friday at 4 pm. The numbers were scribbled on pieces of paper, folded, and exchanged. One of us would smile victoriously, while the other might groan in jest—the one with the lower business figures had the delightful task of treating the other to any ice cream delight on the menu.

This weekly ritual was more than just a simple indulgence; it was a source of motivation, camaraderie, and trust. It symbolised our deep gratitude for each other's support and the shared journey we were on. Regardless of whether the numbers were high or low, we cherished the opportunity to come together, reflect on our progress, and recharge for the week ahead. This ritual not only reinforced our business partnership but also deepened our personal bond.

Moreover, this experience taught us a valuable lesson about the power of self-created gratification. While external recognition is undoubtedly gratifying, we realised that true fulfilment comes from within. By proactively designing rituals and strategies for regular gratification, we expressed gratitude for the blessings in our lives and took ownership of our happiness and success. It wasn't just about the ice cream; it was about the shared moments of triumph, the laughter, and the unwavering support we offered each other.

Like the analogy of planting seeds in a garden, we sow the seeds with the hope of a bountiful harvest, but we also derive satisfaction from witnessing the growth of each sapling, the blossoming of every flower. Similarly, in business, while the ultimate goal may be long-term success, it is crucial to cherish the milestones along the way, no matter how small they may seem.

In essence, our weekly ice cream ritual epitomised the essence of gratification in business—it's not just about the end result but also about the journey, the camaraderie, and the shared experiences. It taught us the importance of celebrating progress, no matter how incremental, and fostering a culture of appreciation and mutual support.

It's important to distinguish between immediate and delayed gratification and understand their roles in our journey. Immediate gratification provides instant pleasure or satisfaction, such as the joy of an ice cream treat after a hard week's work. It's crucial for maintaining motivation and morale, offering short-term rewards that keep us energised. These moments of instant joy and satisfaction can be powerful motivators, driving us to continue putting in the effort and enjoying the journey.

On the other hand, delayed gratification involves postponing immediate rewards for the sake of achieving long-term goals. This might mean investing time and resources into a project that won't pay off for months or even years. Delayed gratification requires patience and foresight, recognising that enduring short-term sacrifices can lead to greater rewards in the future. For example, diligently working on a comprehensive business strategy might not provide immediate results, but it lays the groundwork for sustained success.

Balancing immediate and delayed gratification is essential in business. While immediate gratification keeps the team motivated and engaged, delayed gratification ensures we're working towards significant, long-term achievements. Both are necessary for creating a fulfilling and successful business environment.

The concept of immediate gratification can be expanded further to include various forms of recognition and reward systems within a business. These systems are not only about monetary rewards but also about acknowledging the efforts and achievements of team members. For instance, creating an environment where accomplishments are celebrated through awards, recognition programmes, or even simple gestures like a thank-you note, can significantly boost morale. These acts of recognition are immediate gratifications that reinforce positive behaviour and encourage continued effort.

Delayed gratification, on the other hand, is about strategic planning and long-term vision. It involves setting goals that may take years to achieve but are crucial for the sustained success of the business. This could include investments in employee development, innovation, or infrastructure that might not yield immediate results but are essential for future growth. Encouraging a culture that values long-term planning and perseverance can help build a resilient and enduring business.

Gratitude

Gratitude, alongside gratification, forms the bedrock of purpose in our business. Acknowledging those who have contributed to our journey—family, friends, clients, mentors, and coaches alike—is crucial. Even as we surpass their influence, gratitude keeps us humble, motivating us to pay it forward. In this journey of learning and growth, fostering a culture of appreciation binds us together, making our business more fulfilling and purposeful.

Gratitude is easily forgotten until we take time to pause and reflect on where we are or what someone has done for us last week, last month, or even years ago. Little moments of help are often overlooked. To the receiver, hearing, *"Oh my, I made a difference and am being remembered for it,"* is music to the ears. That effect is unbelievably sweet and impactful. Making a difference, remembering it, and sharing it back makes the whole ecosystem of love and memory more meaningful.

People who know me well know that my mentor took me under his wings and taught me everything I know about the business, despite not being from my own team. We were selfless towards each other. Without him, I would probably never have made it to MDRT. He gave me the MDRT handouts in the 90s and the big blue book and said, *"Read."* He took the time to help me through the business, and for that, I am grateful to him. I have expressed my gratitude to him many times, but I can never say enough how instrumental he has been to me in my business. Many who know me know that I talk about him often. He left a legacy in me, and that's what matters. I am truly grateful to him.

I have taken that experience and helped many people outside my team and in my inner circle to get better and grow. In turn, they have come to me to say thank you, and many have gone on to help others, passing it forward. That's what we are in the business for—making for a better tomorrow. Never shy away from sharing your gratitude for what others have done for you.

Remember, the little things that matter and the little steps others have placed in our journey have made us who we are. So, let's continue to spread the love around.

A key element of gratitude is recognising the contributions of our clients. Their trust in our services is the foundation of our success. I recall a client who faced significant challenges in their business. We worked closely, developing strategies and solutions tailored to their needs. Months later, they sent a heartfelt letter expressing their gratitude for our unwavering support and dedication. That letter became a cherished reminder of the impact we have on others' lives. It reinforced our commitment to excellence and the importance of building genuine relationships.

Gratitude also extends to our team members. They are the backbone of our operations, and acknowledging their efforts is vital. Implementing an employee recognition programme has been transformative for us. Monthly awards for outstanding performance, handwritten notes of appreciation, and celebrating personal milestones have fostered a positive and motivated work environment. These gestures, though small, have a profound impact on morale and productivity.

Furthermore, gratitude has been instrumental in navigating challenges. Maintaining a grateful mindset during difficult times, such as economic downturns or unexpected setbacks, helps us stay resilient. It shifts our focus from what we lack to what we have, enabling us to find creative solutions and remain optimistic. For instance, during a challenging financial period, we expressed our gratitude to clients for their loyalty by offering personalised discounts and enhanced services. This not only strengthened client relationships but also helped us weather the storm.

In the broader community, gratitude drives our social responsibility initiatives. We believe in giving back to the community that supports us. Our team regularly participates in volunteer activities, and we allocate a portion of our profits to charitable organisations. These actions stem from a deep gratitude for our opportunities and a desire to make a positive impact. Witnessing the joy and gratitude of those we help reinforces our commitment to social responsibility, and strengthens our sense of purpose.

Gratification and gratitude dovetail beautifully, creating a cycle of positivity and progress. Gratification celebrates achievements and motivates us to strive for more, while gratitude keeps us grounded, reminding us of the contributions and support of others. This balance ensures that we remain humble in success and resilient in adversity.

The interplay of gratification and gratitude has also been evident in our mentorship programmes. I have had the privilege of mentoring numerous individuals, guiding them through their professional journeys. Seeing their growth and success is immensely gratifying. One of my mentees, who initially struggled with self-confidence, blossomed into a confident and capable leader. Her journey reminded me of my own beginnings and the invaluable support I received from my mentor. This cycle of giving and receiving support perpetuates a culture of growth and mutual respect.

In another instance, a young entrepreneur approached me for advice. He was passionate but lacked direction. Over several months, we worked together to develop his business plan, refine his strategies, and build his network. His transformation was remarkable. He often expressed his gratitude for my guidance, and his success was a testament to the power of mentorship. This experience reinforced the importance of paying it forward and the lasting impact of genuine support and encouragement.

Moreover, integrating gratitude into our daily operations has led to a more cohesive and motivated team. We start our weekly meetings with a *"gratitude round"*, where team members share something they are grateful for, whether personal or professional. This practice fosters a positive atmosphere and strengthens our connections. It reminds us of the bigger picture and the collective effort that drives our success.

Gratitude can also be formalised through structured recognition programmes. Such programmes can include employee of the month awards, public acknowledgements during meetings, or even a dedicated appreciation day. These formal recognitions create a culture where gratitude is not only expressed but institutionalised, ensuring that appreciation is a consistent part of the business environment.

Another practical application of gratitude is in client relationship management. Regularly reaching out to clients to thank them for their business and to check in on their satisfaction can strengthen relationships and enhance loyalty. Personalised messages, whether handwritten notes or customised emails, can make clients feel valued and appreciated, fostering a deeper connection with the business.

Gratitude extends beyond interpersonal interactions to encompass corporate social responsibility (CSR). Businesses that give back to their communities demonstrate gratitude for the support they receive and contribute to the well-being of society. CSR initiatives can include charitable donations, employee volunteer programmes, or partnerships with non-profit organisations. These efforts not only benefit the community but also enhance the company's reputation and build goodwill.

The benefits of gratitude are not limited to external relationships; they also impact internal operations. A culture of gratitude can improve employee retention, boost morale, and increase productivity. When employees feel appreciated and recognised for their contributions, they are more likely to be engaged and committed to their work. This positive work environment can lead to higher levels of job satisfaction and overall business success.

Conclusion

As we look to the future, the principles of gratification and gratitude will continue to guide us. They are not just abstract concepts but practical tools that shape our interactions, decisions, and strategies. By embracing these principles, we create a sustainable and fulfilling business environment where everyone feels valued and motivated.

Thus, with a balance of gratification and gratitude, we pave the way for a better tomorrow. Embracing these principles not only enhances our professional lives but also contributes to our personal growth and well-being. As we continue to navigate the challenges and opportunities of the financial advisory profession, let us remember the power of gratitude and gratification in shaping a brighter future for ourselves and those around us.

Epilogue
Turning Knowledge Into Action

As you reach the end of this book, take a moment to reflect on what you have learned. The strategies, principles, and stories shared in these pages are more than just knowledge—they are a call to action. Success in the financial profession is not a matter of chance; it is a matter of choice—the choice to learn, to grow, and to persist in the face of challenges.

The Power of Implementation

Knowledge without action is meaningless. The insights you have gained from this book will only be valuable if you put them into practice. Think about the areas of your practice that need improvement. What steps can you take today to apply what you have learned?

Start small. Whether it is implementing a new client engagement strategy, refining your personal branding, or exploring advanced planning techniques, the key is to begin. Small, consistent actions lead to significant results over time.

The Role of Relationships

At its core, the financial profession is about relationships. The trust you build with your clients, the partnerships you form with your peers, and the connections you foster within your community all contribute to your success.

As you implement the lessons from this book, remember that your impact extends beyond numbers. You have the power to change lives, provide security and confidence, and help your clients achieve their dreams.

Building a Legacy

Success is not just about what you achieve; it is about what you leave behind. As you grow your practice, think about the legacy you want to create. How will you ensure that the success you build endures beyond your career?

The chapters on succession planning and legacy provide practical guidance on how to plan for the future. By taking proactive steps today, you can ensure that your impact continues for generations to come.

The Journey Ahead

The journey to success is never over. It is a continuous process of learning, adapting, and striving for excellence. This book has equipped you with the tools to navigate that journey, but the path is yours to walk.

Success is not a solo endeavour. Seek out mentors, collaborate with peers, and continue to learn from those who have achieved greatness. Surround yourself with people who inspire and challenge you to be your best.

Your Potential Is Limitless

The financial profession offers unparalleled opportunities for growth, impact, and fulfilment. The principles in this book have been designed to help you unlock those opportunities and realise your full potential.

As you move forward, remember that the measure of your success is not just in what you achieve but in the lives you touch. The journey to greatness is not easy, but it is worth it. The possibilities are limitless, and your potential is boundless.

The next chapter of your journey starts now.

www.ingramcontent.com/pod-product-compliance
Lightning Source LLC
Chambersburg PA
CBHW061141220326
41599CB00025B/4310

* 9 7 8 1 0 3 7 0 4 4 1 3 7 *